"Packed with an abundance of fun ideas, simple [...] *Alchemy* shows you how to grow a great garden from the ground up. From nourishing the soil with organic amendments to crafting custom fertilizers, foliar sprays, and teas, Stephanie's recipes are inspired by the bounty of natural ingredients provided by Mother Nature. There are also plenty of fun projects for all levels of gardeners with ideas for crafting handy items like seed tapes and seed bombs to creating habitats for bees and butterflies. This book is ideal for food and flower gardeners, or anyone who wants to grow a greener garden."

—Niki Jabbour, 2019 American Horticultural Society Award–winning author and longtime radio host of *The Weekend Gardener*

"In her new colorful book, Stephanie Rose nails the simplicity and magic of soil science—making it easy for gardeners to use what's on hand—from common plants to other biomass to grow in ideal conditions. Readers will now have the wisdom they need to create healthy and fertile soil for their gardens!"

—Jessi Bloom, best-selling author, CPH, ECP, ISA arborist, and owner of NW Bloom Ecological Services

"*Garden Alchemy* is full of crafty, thrifty, and *fun* DIY projects that will keep your garden thumb green all year long. I especially appreciate her nod to organics and sustainability throughout the book. Buy this book and get growing!"

—Mark Highland, President, Organic Mechanics Soil Company, and author of *Practical Organic Gardening*

"Stephanie has nailed it with her recipes for growing a healthier garden. The steps for making teas to compost to pest controls are perfect for both the beginner and seasoned gardeners. I can't wait to cook some up to use on my flower farm!"

—Lisa Mason Ziegler, commercial farmer at The Gardeners Workshop, and renowned author, instructor, and expert on cut-flower farming

"As someone who's made a career out of growing in small urban spaces, Stephanie's *Garden Alchemy* is a treasure trove of creative, DIY recipes to grow healthier, stronger plants, beautify your garden, and cultivate more biodiversity in your yard."

—Kevin Espiritu, founder of Epic Gardening and author of *Field Guide to Urban Gardening*

"This book needs to be on every gardener's shelf! In it Stephanie Rose shares recipes for natural soil amendments and fertilizers that will help transform backyards into thriving oases. Using readily available materials—often those that would end up in the landfill—to improve our gardens allows us to close the loop and eliminate the packaging waste that comes with retail solutions. Her recipes for nontoxic solutions to common garden problems take it a step further by replacing harsh pesticides with eco-friendly, healthier alternatives."

—Kris Bordessa, author of *Attainable Sustainable: The Lost Art of Self-Reliant Living* (National Geographic Books, 2020)

Garden Alchemy

80 RECIPES AND CONCOCTIONS for Organic Fertilizers, Plant Elixirs, Potting Mixes, Pest Deterrents, and More

STEPHANIE ROSE of Garden Therapy

COOL
SPRINGS
PRESS

Inspiring | Educating | Creating | Entertaining

Brimming with creative inspiration, how-to projects, and useful information to enrich your everyday life, Quarto Knows is a favorite destination for those pursuing their interests and passions. Visit our site and dig deeper with our books into your area of interest: Quarto Creates, Quarto Cooks, Quarto Homes, Quarto Lives, Quarto Drives, Quarto Explores, Quarto Gifts, or Quarto Kids.

First Published in 2020 by Cool Springs Press, an imprint of The Quarto Group, 100 Cummings Center, Suite 265-D, Beverly, MA 01915, USA.
T (978) 282-9590 F (978) 283-2742 QuartoKnows.com

Cool Springs Press titles are also available at discount for retail, wholesale, promotional, and bulk purchase. For details, contact the Special Sales Manager by email at specialsales@quarto.com or by mail at The Quarto Group, Attn: Special Sales Manager, 100 Cummings Center, Suite 265-D, Beverly, MA 01915, USA.

24 23 22 21 20   1 2 3 4 5

ISBN: 978-0-7603-6709-4

Digital edition published in 2020

Library of Congress Cataloging-in-Publication Data available

Cover and Interior Design: Laura McFadden
Cover Images: Stephanie Rose
Page Layout and Design: Sporto
Photography: Stephanie Rose

Printed in China

Dedication

To those who love the natural world and so
generously share wisdom to benefit us all—please
keep teaching. We are listening, learning,
and growing with you.

Contents

Introduction

In my early gardening days, I met a man who had a lot of plants, but not a lot of land. He was running a backyard nursery as part of a charitable organization that helped people dealing with addiction gain valuable skills through nursery and landscape work. They tended to local gardens and asked permission to pot up any perennial divisions, which they could then propagate and sell. When we met, he was overrun with perennials in 1-gallon (3.8 L) pots and an impending move to a new location. I offered my sunny front yard as a space to host the plants, and I got to work at digging up the lawn to make fresh, new beds.

Then the plants arrived.

Three hundred 1-gallon (3.8 L) pots with green leaves popping out of the soil. No labels. No flowers. No information whatso-ever on what these plants would become.

As you can imagine, that year I got a crash course in herba-ceous perennials. Without even the faintest idea of their light requirements, water needs, height, habit, or bloom times, I was left to design a garden blindfolded. I started by identifying any leaves that I could and placing them in the right spots in the garden. Hostas were easy to identify, and so I paired any other ornamental, broad-leaved plants together in the shade. I also knew what irises looked like, so I grouped these upright grass-like plants together in the sun. I made patterns and borders of plants with similar leaves and got all three hundred of them in the ground.

Miraculously, the majority survived. I had a few surprises, like when one of the plants kept growing taller and taller and

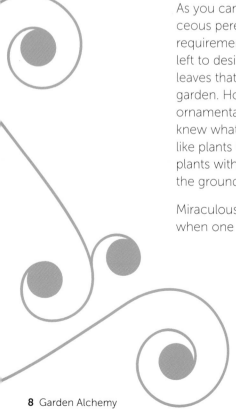

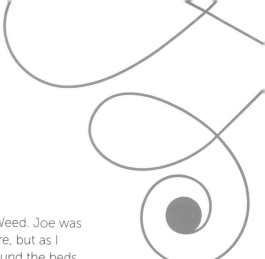

bloomed into a striking eight-foot-tall Joe Pye Weed. Joe was deeply rooted in the soil and not going anywhere, but as I learned, I was able to move the other plants around the beds to find them the space, light, or nourishment they craved.

During my daily garden visits, I listened to what the plants were trying to teach me. Leaf color gave me tips on how they felt about nighttime temperatures and the quality of their soil. Drooping flowers were begging for a cool drink or a spot of shade. They made every effort to grow and only gave up when the conditions provided were too dire for survival. Mostly, they would bounce back after I heard the call and made a change.

It helped me greatly to observe the healthy plants as well, not just the ones who complained. Which ones were thriving, and what did that say about the soil? Weeds are so often admonished for their tenacity, and yet they persist to help us understand the health of the soil. Taproots reach down to break up compacted earth and gather the minerals from the deep, all the while letting us know the topsoil is too compacted and low in fertility for our garden plants.

While I had no idea what I was getting into when I offered up my urban yard, I'm endlessly grateful for what that experience taught me about plants, the soil, and the interconnectedness of nature. My education as a gardener has come from a multitude of sources, from classrooms to field study, all the while bringing the words to life by experimenting in the soil. But by far, the most generous and patient teachers I have ever had have been plants.

What Is Garden Alchemy?

Alchemy's history is shrouded in controversy. Those practicing the art were admonished for tirelessly working on transmutation, famously failing to turn metals into gold. Yet as anyone who has experienced failure knows, alchemists learned a whole lot about the natural world through their experimentation. They hacked natural processes to get a better understanding of how things work, and while their research has been left to many interpretations, the investigational methods they used can be employed to give us a deeper understanding of the natural processes of our gardens.

Alchemists also searched for the universal cure for disease and for longevity, and it is again their inability to meet those lofty goals that teach us more about gardening. Many gardeners have a strong desire to know the exact formula for success for their garden, yet there are endless conflicting studies and opinions out there from PhDs to elders.

So what does that tell us? That there is no magic potion or secret sauce that will grow a perfect garden every time (although compost comes pretty close). The most successful gardeners have learned the formula that works best for them through observation, testing, and time. You can read and study every written word, but, in the end, it's getting your hands dirty that will give you the definitive answer how best to grow plants in your unique garden.

That's where *Garden Alchemy* comes in. Whether you are a brand-new gardener or have many homegrown tomatoes under your belt, this book is full of recipes, concoctions, experiments, and projects for you to play with in your garden. Using nature as a guide, the recipes come from the earth and work to build on the foundation Mother Nature has created.

Get started with *Garden Alchemy* by completing the soil testing recipes in chapter 1. This will help you to get to know your unique garden soil. Then you can go through the recipes like a cookbook, finding those that look interesting to you and giving them a try in your space. Before long, you will have some new favorite natural ideas for growing a lush and thriving garden, along with the confidence that you know what truly works for your individual space.

Soils and Mulches

Learning about your soil is the first step to a healthy and productive garden, and it's a lifelong journey. The soil in your yard may be different than the soil from a prior home. It can be quite different from your neighbor's land. And it can even differ around your property.

While it may seem like the best way to start the gardening journey is to haul in a load of brand spanking new soil and start fresh, that strategy can be fraught with challenges. Bulk topsoil or garden soil can come from a variety of different sources and can contain undesirable things, such as pesticides, herbicides, and plastics. Adding poor quality soil to a garden can cause damage that could take many years to repair.

Even if you do get excellent quality topsoil and the first year of gardening is wildly productive, those easily accessed nutrients will soon be depleted. After that, the new soil will need to be amended annually until it becomes rich with the organic matter and microbes that make up living soil. A much less expensive and productive way to is to start by amending the soil you have. But before you can do that, you need to assess it.

Take some time to meet your soil. Learn about its natural structure, pH, and health. In this chapter, I'll share some simple home tests for evaluating your soil as a foundation for the garden alchemy you will use to grow a healthy, regenerative, and thriving garden. Learning to work with what you have is a skill that will save you time, energy, and money in the long run.

At-Home Soil Testing

A soil test is an important first step in getting to know the soil you are working with. Basic home tests can give you a better understanding of the soil composition and pH, which will serve as a basis for the recipes in this book.

With just a bit of information about your soil, you will begin your relationship with the land, learning about what works and what doesn't work for your space. Some of the plants you grow will effortlessly take root, while others may struggle despite your best efforts. Learning to work with your soil as opposed to fighting its nature will bring the gardener in sync with the garden.

While this strategy works well for many home gardeners, if plant problems are persistent and your efforts are not resolving the issues, lab testing provides a detailed qualitative assessment of your soil, including nutrients, toxins, and microbes.

Simple Squeeze Test

This quick and simple test can be done right in the garden with minimal time or disruption. Take a handful of soil from the garden and squeeze it into a ball. Poke it with your finger and observe the results:

- If it sticks together, it's clay.
- If it falls apart somewhat, it's loam.
- If it falls apart completely, it's sand.

How to Collect a Soil Sample

To collect a soil sample, dig down 3 to 4 inches (7.5 to 10 cm) with a trowel and scoop soil into a bowl. Take three to five samples from different parts of the garden and mix them together. Do not to touch the sample with your hands to avoid altering the pH.

Soil Composition Test in a Mason Jar

Soil is made up of sand, silt, and clay. The ideal balance of these particles for garden soil is called "loam." It is suitable for growing most plants as it has a great balance of air pockets, moisture and nutrient retention, and drainage.

Test It!

Loam is made up of 40 percent sand, 40 percent silt, and 20 percent clay.

- Sand makes up the largest soil particles (between 0.05 to 2 mm in diameter)

- Silt makes up the intermediate size soil particles (between 0.002 to 0.05 mm in diameter)

- Clay makes up the smallest soil particles (smaller than 0.002 mm in diameter)

To determine the mix of soil you have in your garden, fill a 1-quart (1 liter) Mason jar one-third full with garden soil. Fill the rest of the jar with water and close the lid tightly. Shake the jar well. Let the contents settle overnight. In the morning, there will be up to four visible layers from bottom to top: sand, silt, clay, and water.

Water

Clay

Silt

Sand

Results

Measure the percentages of sand, silt, and clay to learn your garden soil's composition. Additionally, the clarity of the water sheds light on soil composition.

- If the water is clear, the soil is primarily free-draining sand.

- If the water is murky with soil suspended, it is loam.

- If the water is murky with visible sediment around the jar, it is mostly clay.

Soil pH Tests

In chemistry, pH measures how acidic or alkaline soil is based on a scale from 0 to 14. A pH of 7 is considered neutral, while values of 0 to 7 indicate acidity and, 7 to 14 indicate alkalinity. Soil pH is typically between 4.5 to 9. Most plants thrive in neutral soil—with a pH near 6.5 to 7—with a few exceptions. Acid-loving plants such as rhododendrons and blueberries prefer a lower pH between 4.5 to 5.5, while others such as asparagus and sweet pea can tolerate a pH slightly above 7. Some plants can tolerate a range of soil pH.

Vinegar and Baking Soda pH Test

This simple test for soil pH will tell you if you have alkaline, acidic, or neutral soil using household vinegar and baking soda. Vinegar is acidic and sodium bicarbonate (baking soda) is alkaline. When they are mixed together, they fizz. With two samples of soil from the same place in your garden, adding these ingredients will help to determine your soil's pH type.

Materials

2 small bowls

4 tablespoons soil

Distilled water (do not use tap water as distilled water has a neutral pH)

White vinegar

Sodium bicarbonate

Make It!

Add 2 tablespoons (30 ml) soil to a small bowl and mix with 1 tablespoon (15 ml) distilled water. Add 1 tablespoon (15 ml) white vinegar and stir. If the mixture fizzes, you have alkaline soil.

Add 2 tablespoons (30 ml) soil from the same sample to a small bowl and mix with 1 tablespoon (15 ml) distilled water. Add 1 tablespoon (15 ml) baking soda and stir. If the mixture fizzes, you have acidic soil. If it does not fizz for either test, you have neutral soil.

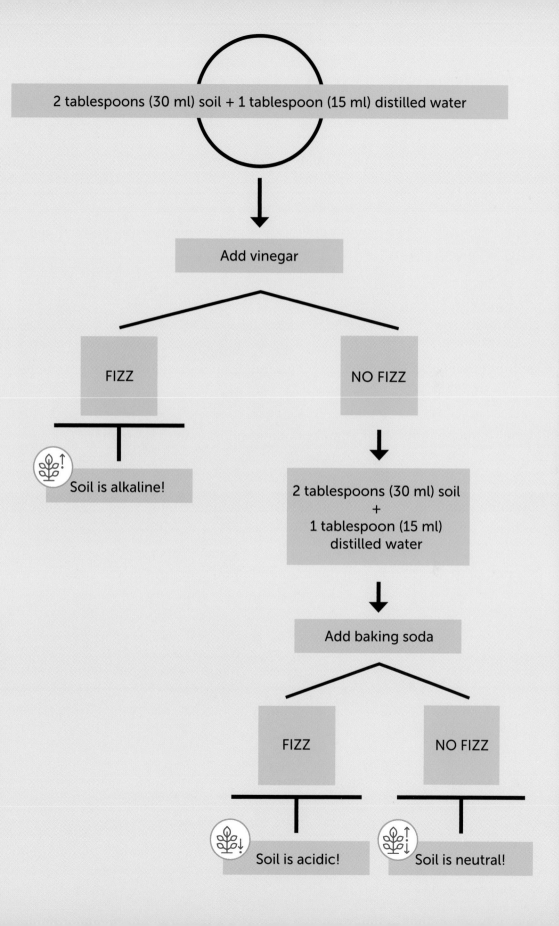

Cabbage Water pH Test

Make a pH indicator solution using red cabbage water in this colorful home test. Water-soluble pigments in cabbage—known as anthocyanins—turn pink to red when mixed with acidic soil, greenish yellow when mixed with alkaline soil, and bluish purple when mixed with neutral soil.

Materials
Saucepan

3 cups (710 ml) distilled water

1 cup (235 ml) finely chopped red cabbage

2 Mason jars

Soil samples

Test It!

1 Bring the distilled water and cabbage to a boil in the saucepan; simmer for 10 minutes. Allow the cabbage water to cool.

2 Add ½ cup (120 ml) of the cabbage water to each Mason jar and stir in 1 tablespoon (15 ml) garden soil. Let the samples sit for thirty minutes before reading the color.

DIY Soil pH Test Kits

There are plenty of soil test kits that you can buy to test soil pH, from electronic meters to paper strips. Each test has its own set of unique instructions and some can also measure sunlight, soil fertility, and moisture levels. The simplest and most economical option is all that is needed at home. Paper pH litmus tests can be purchased inexpensively in books or rolls offering hundreds of tests.

Test It!

1 To use a pH litmus test strip, mix a soil sample with distilled water for 30 seconds.

2 Touch the tip of the test paper to the top of the muddy mixture and hold it in place for one minute.

3 The water will be wicked up by the paper, and the pH reading can be taken from the point closest to the tip that is not covered in mud.

Change Hydrangea Bloom Colors

Hydrangea varieties such as *Hydrangea macrophylla* and *H. serrata* can range in color from pink to blue, with every shade of fuchsia, plum, and periwinkle in between. The blooms can change color based on the amount of aluminum the plants absorb from the soil, which depends on soil pH. High levels of aluminum in the soil plus an acidic soil pH will generate the coveted bright blue to purple flowers, while less aluminum in the soil and/or alkaline soil will create a variation of pink blooms. Not all hydrangea species change color, however. White ones do not change, and some varieties are bred for a specific color palette.

Materials
For blue flowers:
½ cup (120 ml) sulfur per 10 square feet (1 square meter).

For pink flowers:
1 cup (235 ml) garden lime per 10 square feet (1 square meter).

Moody Blues

For blue hues, use soil amendments like elemental sulfur and gypsum, or use an organic fertilizer containing cottonseed meal when feeding the plants. Recommendations to add aluminum sulfate to the soil, are often not necessary and could be harmful. Aluminum is plentiful and not an essential plant nutrient, and too much of it can be toxic.

Make It!

1 Add sulfur or garden lime to alter the pH.

2 Repeat every 3 months for blue flowers and every 2 months for pink flowers.

Changing the pH of your soil is a gradual process that can take up to a year for the color change to happen.

Potting Soil Recipes

Potting soils for container plants are a mix of organic materials that generally do not contain garden soil. Just as not all plants will thrive in all types of garden soil, plants in containers have different soilless mixture needs.

Container gardens confine plant roots to a small amount of soil, limited by the container's size, so the composition of the potting soil should be lightweight and free-draining. Plants will use soil nutrition and water quickly when they're planted in a container, so it's important to include particles that hold onto moisture and nutrients.

For **seed-starting,** create a mix with fine particles, moisture-holding ingredients, and sterile ingredients that won't stimulate fungal or bacterial growth. Seed mixes don't need fertilizer or nutrient mixes as the seed carries all the nutrition that the seedling needs to sprout. Once a plant develops its "true leaves," it's time to pot up the seedlings using a transplant mix, which will keep the plant growing strong until it's ready for the garden. While seed-starting mix is soilless and sterile, once seedlings get growing they are going to need a boost of nutrients to keep them growing.

Like other potted plants and outdoor containers, **houseplants** dry out quickly and need a soil mix that can retain moisture and keep them hydrated. However, unlike outdoor containers, houseplants require sterile soil—anything else is likely to contain critters from the outdoors such as fungus gnats that may get into the house and can become a nuisance.

With the exception of compost, most soil ingredients do not have active biology. Prepare compost for indoor potting soil by baking moist soil in the sun or an oven for at least thirty minutes at 180°F (82°C). Alternatively, you can purchase sterilized compost. Store any leftover compost in an airtight container for future indoor and seed-starting potting mixes.

INGREDIENTS

SYMBOLS LEGEND

 Nutrients – contains nutrients

 Water – holds water in the soil for plant availability

 Drainage – allows water to flow freely

 Air – creates pockets of air in the soil

 Sterile – contains no soil microbes

 Acidic – acidic pH

 pH Neutral – neutral pH

 Byproduct – a waste product that can be repurposed into a potting mix ingredient.

KEY

retains moisture · excellent drainage

Compost

Properly finished and screened compost is the cornerstone of building many potting soils. It is made up of broken-down organic matter that is rich in microorganisms and adds life to soil. Compost holds moisture and allows nutrients to be available to plants; however, quality varies greatly based on the inputs and composting methods.

Both urban and farm compost can be devoid of proper nutrients and contain undesirable materials such as pesticides, herbicides, and plastics. Use properly balanced homemade compost or purchase top-quality commercial compost from a trusted source.

Ground Bark / Bark Fines

Ground bark is byproduct of milling wood. It holds moisture and adds air space to potting mixes. As the bark slowly decomposes, it helps to improve the soil. Bark is sold as both a soil amendment and mulch, so it is available in various sizes. Use finely ground pine bark—also called "bark fines"—between one-quarter to one-half inch in size (.6 cm to 1.3 cm) for soil amending. It's inexpensive and easy to acquire, but it is not recommended for root vegetables and seed mixes that require finer soil particles.

Sphagnum Peat Moss

Sphagnum peat moss is a naturally occurring, moisture-retaining material that is free of plant pathogens, weed seeds, mineral salts, or heavy metals. It aerates clay soil, binds sandy soil, and reduces nutrient leaching, which makes it a popular soil ingredient. Harvesting sphagnum peat moss comes with many sustainability issues that need to be considered (see the sidebar "Sphagnum Peat Moss and Environmental Responsibility").

Sphagnum peat moss is acidic so it should be amended with one tablespoon (15 ml) garden lime per gallon (3.8 liter) to balance out the pH unless you are using it for acid-loving plants, such as blueberries and rhododendrons. When sphagnum peat moss dries, it can make the texture of potting soil stiff and impermeable, making it difficult to rehydrate. The acidic pH, rehydration issue, and sustainability concerns are strong reasons to go with a peat alternative in the home garden.

Coconut Coir

Coconut coir is made from the waste products of coconut husks. It has exceptional water-holding ability, is lightweight, and is often marketed a sustainable alternative to peat moss (see the sidebar "Sphagnum Peat Moss and Environmental Responsibility"). It has a neutral pH but doesn't hold on to nutrients as well.

There is a wide quality range in horticultural coconut coir products; some brands may not perform well in potting soil while others may be a valuable addition. Before making a large investment purchasing any coconut coir, test a few brands to find one that works for you.

Vermiculite

Vermiculite is a naturally occurring group of minerals that has a spongy texture when processed into pellets (chips). It absorbs and holds moisture and aerates the soil structure. Vermiculite has a neutral pH and it is often used in seed-starting mixes. Only horticultural grade vermiculite should be used for potting soils (see the sidebar "Safety").

Rice Hulls

Rice hulls are a byproduct of rice farming. Hulls are the outer husks removed from each grain of rice after harvesting. They are heated and sterilized before being sold as a garden soil conditioner. Rice hulls are lightweight and break down quickly in the garden, usually within one season. They improve drainage, hold water in the soil, and improve aeration. Rice hulls are often inexpensive and can be found at homebrewing supply stores if you do not find them in a garden supply store.

Sand

Sand is fine granular rock that improves drainage when paired with organic materials. Too much sand in soil can affect the soil structure and decrease permeability. Adding sand to clay soils may seem like a good idea, but it's better to add organic matter to adjust soil structure as sand and clay together will "cement" together and further decrease air space. Look for horticultural sand as a potting mix ingredient, as beach sand can contain salt, glass, and plastic.

Perlite

Perlite is a naturally occurring volcanic glass that is highly porous and lightweight. When heated, it puffs up and looks like balls of Styrofoam. It is added to soil to increase drainage and aeration, keeping soil lightweight and free-flowing. It is a good option for a succulent/cactus mix, propagating root cuttings, and container gardening.

Horticultural Pumice

Horticultural pumice, often just referred to as "pumice," is a plentiful volcanic rock that can be added to soils to increase air space and improve drainage. Pumice is lightweight and does not hold water in the soil, so it is suitable for plants that require excellent drainage, such as succulents and cacti. It has similar properties to perlite, but it's heavier, making it more suitable for small pots and tall plants that need more weight at their base for stability.

Safety

Have you ever emptied a bag of soil mix just to be surrounded by a cloud of dust? Inhaling dust and particles can lead to health problems that can be easily avoided by using the proper safety equipment. I always recommend that you wear a mask and gardening gloves when mixing potting soils or using any bagged potting soil. Handling damp or wet soil can also reduce dust and particle inhalation, so add some water to your soil as you mix, fill pots, and plant.

Sphagnum Peat Moss and Environmental Responsibility

Sphagnum peat moss comes from bogs, which make up 3 percent of the earth's total surface. Peat bogs are part of the natural landscape of many countries around the world, with the largest area (approximately 25 percent) of peatlands in Canada. Peat bogs are excellent at absorbing and storing carbon to reduce climate change, and they are also home to many wildlife and plant species, some quite rare. Peat is used around the world as fuel for cooking and heating, and it is considered a slowly renewable fossil fuel that releases more emissions than coal and natural gas. Many countries have overharvested peatlands, which has resulted in protection and conservation efforts in countries throughout the globe.

Canada is the largest producer of Sphagnum peat moss as a soil conditioner. Canada contains 119 million hectares of peatlands and approximately 22,000 hectares are harvested for peat. Peatlands are protected in Canada and the producers must agree to regenerate the land that has been harvested. Even so, harvesting peat bogs releases carbon and displaces wildlife, which take many years to repair.

Coconut coir is promoted as a peat alternative, often being marketed as a "peat" product. There is some debate on whether it is truly more sustainable as the coir needs to be processed, which uses resources and can affect worker health, not to mention the long distances it will travel when shipped to temperate climates.

Many ingredients that are commonly used for home gardens and agriculture, while they are "organic," "natural," and good for building soil, raise sustainability questions and environmental considerations. It's important not to simply replace what we harvest and sustain our natural systems but look to how they can be regenerated. Some materials are plentiful, but it takes a long time to replace them through natural growth cycles. Removing them may change the biodiversity and harm ecosystems. The supply of some materials is finite, and while plentiful now, once they are used, they cannot be renewed. The distance that materials travel, the processes used for packaging them, and the reduction of their functions in the natural landscape must all be considered with each material we bring into our garden. Investigate the supply chain before you buy to learn how the materials are sourced, harvested, and prepared to ensure they are in line with your values.

The best practice is to use what you have, glean waste, use byproducts, and acquire materials locally where possible. Just reducing the plastic bags that pre-mixed potting soils come in is progress. Buy local, in bulk, and build your own potting mixes to grow a wonderful garden to feed your body, wildlife, and the earth.

Recipes

Seed-Starting Mix

Seed-starting mix is sterile, offers balanced moisture retention and drainage, and has fine particles to allow seedlings to easily root.

2 parts screened and sterilized compost

2 parts peat moss alternative

1 part perlite

1 part vermiculite

Peat Moss Alternative

This recipe is made up of byproducts and therefore is a more eco-friendly alternative to peat. It is also pH neutral and doesn't dry out like peat, making it a superior option for potting soil.

1 part compost

1 part coconut coir

1 part rice hulls or perlite

Seedling Transplant Mix

A seedling transplant mix has excellent drainage and available nutrients for developing healthy roots on young plants and propagating cuttings.

2 parts screened compost

1 part peat moss alternative

1 part perlite

¼ cup (60 ml) worm castings per each gallon (3.8 L) of prepared mix

Note: If the seedlings are moved to the garden in a few weeks after potting up, then this recipe is sufficient. But if you need to grow them in small pots for a longer period, they will need more nutrition. Bump the worm castings up to ½ cup (120 ml) per gallon (3.8 L) and apply an all-purpose liquid fertilizer every 2 weeks when watering.

All-Purpose Soil Mix

Use this all-purpose soil mix in container gardens, raised beds, and for potting up seedlings. This recipe is useful if you have a variety of different potting mix needs.

2 parts screened compost

2 parts peat moss alternative

1 part perlite

1 cup (235 ml) worm castings per each gallon (3.8 L) of prepared mix

1 tablespoon (15 ml) greensand per each gallon (3.8 L) of prepared mix

1 tablespoon (15 ml) mineralized rock dust per each gallon (3.8 L) of prepared mix

1 tablespoon (15 ml) kelp meal per each gallon (3.8 L) of prepared mix

Acid-Loving Plant Mix

Blueberries, azaleas, and heathers will love this lower pH soil mix.

2 parts compost

1 part finely ground pine bark

1 part sand

1 tablespoon (15 ml) coffee grounds per each gallon (3.8 L) of prepared mix

Cacti and Succulent Mix

Succulents and cacti thrive in dry environments and require the soil to dry out completely between waterings. The best soil for them is made up of light, airy materials with excellent drainage.

1 part compost

1 part ground bark

1 part sand

1 part pumice

Basket Mix

This moisture-holding, nutritious, and lightweight soil mix is perfect for hanging baskets. Line hanging baskets with a coconut coir insert to further retain moisture.

2 parts compost

1 part perlite

1 part vermiculite

1 part worm castings

3 tablespoons (45 ml) blood or alfalfa meal per each gallon (3.8 L) of prepared mix

1 tablespoon (15 ml) kelp meal per each gallon (3.8 L) of prepared mix

Indoor Plant Mix

Use this mix for indoor tropical plants. Ensure that the ingredients you use are sterile to avoid introducing plant pests and disease.

2 parts sterilized compost

2 parts peat moss alternative

1 part worm castings

1 part perlite

1 part vermiculite

1 part sand

Lawn Mix

After seeding your lawn, spread this mix over the seed or use it to fill in uneven spots.

2 parts finely screened compost

1 part sand

Raised Bed Vegetable Mix

To produce the largest (and tastiest!) harvest possible, vegetable plants need lots of nutrients and humus-rich soil.

3 parts compost

1 perlite or rice hulls

1 part sand

¼ cup (60 ml) worm castings per each gallon (3.8 L) of prepared mix

1 tablespoon (15 ml) greensand per each gallon (3.8 L) of prepared mix

1 tablespoon (15 ml) mineralized rock dust per each gallon (3.8 L) of prepared mix

1 tablespoon (15 ml) kelp meal per each gallon (3.8 L) of prepared mix

Epiphyte / Orchid Mix

Epiphytes such as orchids use potting soil as an anchor for their roots, so it should be loose, airy, and with excellent drainage.

4 parts finely ground pine bark

2 parts peat moss alternative

1 part perlite or pumice

Frugal Mix

Potting mix ingredients can add up to more than just great plants. Save a bundle by crafting your own potting mix out of ingredients that you have at home or can purchase inexpensively.

2 parts garden soil

2 parts homemade compost

1 part sand

1 cup (235 ml) rice hulls per each gallon (3.8 L) of prepared mix

1 cup (235 ml) dried, ground seaweed per each gallon (3.8 L) of prepared mix

Woody Plants and Perennial Mix

Woody plants and perennials like a soil mix that breaks down slowly and balances moisture retention with good drainage.

2 parts compost

2 parts finely ground pine bark

1 part perlite or pumice

1 part sand

1 part mushroom manure (compost)

Organic Mulches for Every Garden

Mulching is highly lauded as an essential part of soil insulation, deterring weeds, retaining soil moisture, and nourishing the soil. This wisdom comes straight from the forest. Plant materials such as leaves, bark, and seeds drop to the ground in forests and other wild spaces, where they create a carpet of plant material that decomposes to nourish and build up the soil below. In home gardens, we are taught to remove the plant debris that creates this carpet, and we are then left with bare soil around our plants that dries out quickly and invites weeds to take up residence. Mulching replaces this essential layer in the garden.

There are many different organic mulches that work well for various styles of gardens. Synthetic options like plastic, landscape fabric, and bark that has been dyed for aesthetics should be avoided. The inorganic nature of these materials is rife with problems that will ultimately harm soil, plants, and the ecology.

MULCH MATERIAL	DESCRIPTION	GOOD FOR	AVOID	NOTES
COMPOST	Properly finished and screened compost from the home garden or trusted commercial products. Compost as mulch will slowly leach beneficial nutrients and microbes into the soil through watering.	All gardens	Unfinished compost. Unknown source inputs. Some municipal waste-derived compost.	Homemade compost is free. Compost is readily available.
LEAF MOLD	Leaves are collected and shredded into mulch with a lawnmower or leaf blower on the mulch setting. Leaf mold breaks down quickly and has a high bacterial content.	Vegetables	Diseased or pest-infested leaves. Leaves sprayed with pesticides and herbicides.	Free. Readily available.

WOOD CHIPS	Wood chips from arborists or commercial sources make a great, all-purpose mulch for shrubs, trees, and perennial gardens that don't need to be planted annually. Wood chips feed fungi, which is beneficial to long-term growers.	Perennials		Inexpensive. Readily available.
ROCKS	River stone, gravel, volcanic rock	Xeriscapes	Rock mulch under trees means leaves to pick out of the rocks.	Holds and radiates heat and cold.
PINE STRAW	Pine needles and pinecones make attractive and readily available mulch.	Woodland gardens		Does not affect soil pH as commonly rumored.
STRAW	Utilitarian mulch offering good winter protection.	Homesteads	Hay can contain weed seeds.	
CARD-BOARD	Shredded or torn cardboard pieces that protect soil from nutrient loss.	Rainy climates	Full sheets that can smother soil.	Slow to break down. Remove in dry seasons.
GRASS CLIPPINGS	Allow grass clippings to remain on the lawn as mulch.	Lawns		Grasscycling allows the grass to grow long and go to seed before cutting.
LIVING MULCH	Carpet gardening using low-growing groundcovers under and between plants.	Ornamental gardens		
CHOP AND DROP	Drop plant material on the garden floor and allow it to naturally compost.	Regenerative gardens		Some plants can be specifically grown as mulch.
SNOW	Insulate garden beds with snow. A naturally occurring snowfall can provide winter insulation but is best combined with an all-weather mulch.	Cold climate gardens	Tender plants	
AQUATIC PLANTS	Chop and drop fast-growing aquatic plants as mulch where they will not reseed or take root.	Dry land gardens		
SEAWEED	Shredded seaweed as mulch for plants that naturally grow near oceans.	Coastal gardens	Adding too much seaweed causing plant salt injury.	
SHEET MULCHING	Adding layers of carbon and nitrogen like paper, bark, leaves, and vegetation to compost in place.	Soil creation		Lasagna gardening and Hugelkultur methods for new soil creation.

Propagation

Propagating plants is a great way to start a low-cost, customized garden. Propagating plants *properly* is even better because you start with healthy, organic plantlings that grow into robust and resistant plants.

When the seed catalogs are delivered in winter is the best time to curl up by the fire and start planning your garden. The varieties of plants that are available to start from seed are much more diverse than what you can purchase as nursery starts. With homegrown seedlings, you know the ingredients that go into the plants from the start.

Learning the steps to grow from seeds or plant cuttings is an important part of your education as a plant parent. It helps to see both the fragility and strength of plants contained in a small scale. Propagation can be one of the most difficult parts of growing a garden, but it is also one of the most rewarding. If you can learn to provide the proper conditions for plants to germinate and take root, then you will be another step closer to your connection to the garden.

There are plenty of recipes and projects in this chapter that make propagation easy and a whole lot of fun! Now let's get the (garden) party started with seed-starting, seed bombing, and propagating from cuttings.

Seed Germination Test

Packaged seeds are tested for their germination rates (the percentage of seeds that will sprout). Germination rates decline as seeds age, vary by variety, and can be altered by storage conditions and other factors. Newly purchased seeds do not need germination testing, but if you have seeds that are many years old or that you have collected yourself, then a seed germination test will save you the effort of planting seeds that aren't going to germinate.

Materials
10 seeds
Paper towel
Plastic bag
Spray bottle
Label

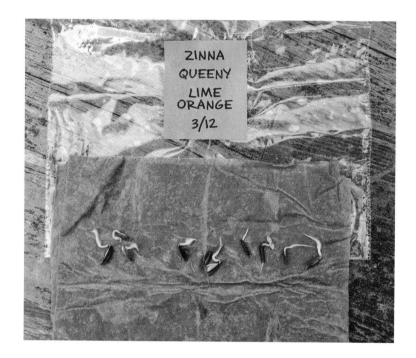

Make It!

1 Fold a paper towel in half and wet it with a spray bottle of water.

Place the 10 seeds inside the fold of the paper towel, and cover.

2 Place the paper towel in the plastic bag (it can be folded) and close the bag partly to create a mini greenhouse. (The bag needs to have a bit of airflow so keep part of it open.) Label the bag with the seed variety and date.

3 Set the bag in a warm spot such as on top of the refrigerator.

4 Each day check the seeds for signs of sprouting and mist the paper towel. Seeds should sprout within 3 to 10 days, or as indicated for the variety.

If germination rates are low (less than 85 percent), plant extra seeds or, if it's quite low, compost the seeds altogether and purchase new ones.

Recycled Seed-Starting Pots

Using what you have available is a great way to make recycled seed-starting pots and reduces waste.

Newspaper Pots

Newspaper pots are sturdy enough to handle holding seeds while they germinate, and they break down readily in the garden.

To make them, wrap 3½-inch x 12-inch (8.5-cm x 30-cm) strips of newspaper around a paper pot maker or small tomato paste can, leaving an extra 1 to 2 inches (30 to 60 cm) of newspaper hanging past the bottom of the cylinder. Fold the overhanging newspaper in toward the middle of the base to create a bottom for your seedling pot.

Toilet Tissue Pots

Toilet tissue pots are a bit sturdier and work well for cuttings and seeds that take longer to germinate.

To make them, cut the toilet paper roll in half and then cut four ½-inch-long (1-cm-long) slits on the bottom of one end, equally spaced to make four flaps you will fold over like closing a box.

The cardboard will take longer to break down in a garden than the seedling's rootball will grow, so gently tear each pot to remove it and toss them in the compost bin at planting time.

Cardboard Egg Carton Starter for Peas and Greens

Cardboard egg cartons are great for starting shallow-rooted plants such as peas and lettuces that you would normally plant in a row.

Use a box cutter to score (but don't cut all the way through) a line through the middle of all six cells on each side of the carton, on the bottom, parallel to the longest side of the carton. The idea is that the cells stay together when the

seeds germinate, but they can easily be split apart when planting. Set the cells into the lid, using it as a tray to hold it all together. Fill the cells with seed-starting soil mix and plant the seeds.

When transplanting time comes around, cut the bottom of the carton (the cells) in half lengthwise so you have two rows of six seedlings. Make a trough in the garden soil where you intend to plant and break the cardboard apart where you scored it so that the seedlings fall through the bottom into the trough.

Soil-Blocking Tool

A soil-blocking tool is the least wasteful of all of these options because it requires no additional materials. A soil blocker is used to press seed-starting potting mix into blocks that hold their shape for seed germination.

To make a tray of soil blocks, combine the seed-starting mix with water in a wide bin until it is the texture of wet sand; it should hold together when you squeeze it into a ball. Press the soil-blocking tool into the wet seed-starting mix, lift the tool over to a seed tray, and press the handle to release the blocks.

Mini Greenhouse

A mini greenhouse made from a clear plastic container allows seedlings to get enough light while holding in humidity to help germination. Recycled salad boxes work wonderfully, but you can choose any food-safe, clear plastic container that has a lid to hold in moisture.

Make this mini greenhouse by choosing a plastic box with a lid that works for you. Plant seeds directly into soil in the tray, or set newspaper pots, toilet tissue pots, or soil blocks in the tray. Cut a few holes in the lid for airflow. Remove the lid daily to allow air exchange, and water the seedlings from the bottom to prevent disrupting them. Remove the lid completely when the seedlings emerge and place the greenhouse in bright light.

Seed Bombs

Making seed bombs is a fun project to get the whole family thinking about how we can help the earth by renewing growth in barren landscapes. These seed bombs are simple to make and they are a creative handmade gift idea.

There are two basic recipes to make seed bombs: clay-based and paper-based. Both follow a similar method of creating a binding mix that sticks together when wet and which hardens to hold the seeds in place (until water is added later).

Create your own seed mix with a combination of annuals, biennials, and perennials for a garden that blooms in the first year and for many more.

How Many Seeds?

Seeds come in all shapes and sizes. As do plants. And plant spacing. So how do you know how many seeds to add to a seed bomb?

A pinch!

As a general rule of thumb, each seed bomb should contain a "pinch" of seeds, the number you can easily pick up with your thumb and forefinger. For larger seeds such as sunflowers and pumpkins, this could be just two seeds, but for smaller seeds such as poppies or lettuce, it could be ten seeds.

Press larger seeds right into the middle of the seed bomb. Smaller seeds can be mixed right into the basic recipe, and a few can even be pressed onto the outside of the seed bomb. The odds are that not all of the seeds will germinate as this form of guerilla gardening is a much looser way of planting than what's recommended on a seed packet. Adding a few extra seeds and a variety of different seeds ensure that the seed bomb will have the best chance of growing into beautiful plants.

Clay-Based Seed Bomb Recipe

Clay-based seed bombs are a great way to get your hands dirty! They are made up of just four ingredients—powdered clay, compost, water, and seeds—making them approachable and fun to make for kids of all ages. Adding a few pretty seeds and dried flower petals to the outside makes them as decorative as they are functional. For example, *Calendula* seeds are curly, sunflowers have stripes, marigold seeds look like little porcupine quills, and *Centaurea* seeds look like gold and gray rockets. A variety of mixed seeds could look quite decorative.

Materials

5 parts finely screened compost

1 part bentonite clay (or substitute for another color of powdered clay)

Water

Seeds

Make It!

1   Mix the compost and bentonite clay in a bowl or bucket and add just enough water to make the mixture hold together.

2   Form into balls and add a pinch of seeds. Large seeds can be pushed into the middle of the ball while smaller seeds can be dispersed throughout the mix. Roll the ball between the palms of your hands to compact it and get a nice round shape.

3   If desired, roll the ball in a tray of dried flower petals, such as rose, calendula, and bachelor's button, or add a few attractive seeds to the outside.

4   Set the seed balls on a tray in a cool, dry place out of direct sunlight to harden. The seed bombs have dried when they no longer feel cool to the touch and are quite hard.

Paper-Based Seed Bomb Recipe

Paper seed bombs open up a world of color options, and they are a lot less messy than the clay-based recipe. Plus, you can recycle a material that you surely have a lot of—paper! These bombs can be pressed into candy molds or ice cube trays for unique shapes.

Materials

Makes 12 ice cube-sized seed bombs.

8–10 sheets white paper

1–2 sheets dyed tissue paper

Water

Immersion blender with jar

Dish towel

Bowl

Seeds

Ice cube tray or candy mold

Make It!

1 Shred the paper using a paper shredder, scissors, or by hand. The paper can be printed with black or colored ink, but the more ink is used, the more it will affect the color of the seed bomb. A sheet or two of dyed tissue paper adds color to the seed bombs. Avoid using waxy paper, plastic envelope windows, or paper with staples.

2 Add the shredded paper to the immersion blender jar and pour in warm water to cover the paper. Allow the paper to sit in the water for 10 minutes to soften. Use the immersion blender to turn the paper into pulp until it is the consistency of oatmeal.

3 Set an open dish towel over a bowl large enough to capture all the excess water and pour the paper pulp into the center of the towel. Squeeze the towel to remove as much of the water as possible.

4 Mix the paper pulp with the seeds, approximately ¼ teaspoon (1 ml) or 12 pinches of small seeds, using your hands. Press the pulp and seeds into an ice cube tray or candy mold.

(continued on page 40)

5

6

5 Remove extra moisture from the pulp by pressing the molded mixture with a dry dish towel. Press firmly. This speeds up drying time and discourages seed germination.

6 Carefully remove the bombs from the mold and set on a board to dry.

Be the Birds

Many native plant species depend on birds and other animals to help spread their seeds. Tasty berries are gobbled up by our feathered friends who digest the sweet fruit and deposit the seeds some distance away from the source.

Even though the birds do it, please don't start bombing your neighborhood and parks with seeds! The idea of this fun project is to help reintroduce species where they would have grown naturally. The best practice is to make seed bombs using native plants that grow well in your area. Many seed companies sell wildflower and pollinator mixes that are perfectly suited for seed bombs. Source seeds from a local seed company that specializes in the species of plants that thrive in your area. Trusted seed companies will not sell invasive species that could damage habitat. A little bit of research about the plants that are best for seed bombing in your area will go a long way.

Bombs Away!

If you thought making seed bombs was fun, wait until you plant them! Seed bombs are ideal for planting in large or hard-to-reach spaces such as meadows and ditches. Throw them far and try to hit solid ground; a slingshot can really send them flying.

Ideally, the bomb will break apart upon contact, but that's not necessary for the seeds to grow. Flat-bottomed seeds will be able to stay on a hillside, while round balls can roll into hard to reach places. Have fun with planting and be sure to visit in a few weeks or months to see the fruits (or flowers) of your labor.

Seed Bomb Recipes

Pollinator Party

Anise Hyssop (*Agastache* 'Blue Fortune')
Annual Baby's Breath (*Gypsophila elegans*)
Bachelor's Button (*Centaurea cyanus*)
Borage (*Borago officinalis*)
Butterfly Weed (*Asclepias tuberosa*)
Common Milkweed (*Asclepias syriaca*)
Rocky Mountain Bee Plant (*Cleome serrulata*)
Spider Flower (*Cleome hassleriana*)
Wild Bergamot / Bee Balm (*Monarda fistulosa*)

Bee Blend

Bee Balm (*Monarda* spp.)
Black-Eyed Susan (*Rudbeckia hirta*)
Crimson Clover (*Trifolium incarnatum*)
French Lavender (*Lavandula stoechas*)
Lanceleaf Coreopsis (*Coreopsis lanceolate*)
Purple Coneflower (*Echinacea purpurea*)
Sunflower (*Helianthus annuus*)
Zinna (*Zinnia elegans, Z. angustifolia*)

Sweet Nectar Plants

Anise Hyssop (*Agastache* 'Blue Fortune')
Bee Balm (*Monarda* spp.)
Butterfly Weed (*Asclepias tuberosa*)
Cosmos (*Cosmos bipinnatus*)
French Lavender (*Lavandula stoechas*)
Faassens Catnip (*Nepeta faasenii*)
Salvia (*Salvia coccinea*)
Zinna (*Zinnia elegans, Z. angustifolia*)

Got the Blues

Baby Blue Eyes (*Nemophila menziesii*)
Bachelor's Button (*Centaurea cyanus*)
Blue Flax (*Linum lewisii*)
Borage (*Borago officinalis*)
Forget-Me-Not (*Myosotis sylvatica*)
Love-in-a-Mist (*Nigella damascena*)

Cheery Annuals

Bachelor's Button (*Centaurea cyanus*)
Calendula (*Calendula officinalis*)
California Poppy (*Eschscholzia californica*)
Cosmos (*Cosmos bipinnatus, C. suphureus*)
Lupine (*Lupinus* spp.)
Marigold (*Tagetes* spp.)
Sunflower (*Helianthus annuus*)
Sweet Pea (*Lathryrus odoratus*)
Zinna (*Zinnia elegans, Z. angustifolia*)

Meadow Flowers

Bachelor's Button (*Centaurea cyanus*)
Blue Flax (*Linum lewisii*)
Poppy (*Papaver* spp.)
Cosmos (*Cosmos* spp.)
Hollyhocks (*Alcea* spp.)
Love-in-a-Mist (*Nigella damascena*)
Prairie Coneflower (*Ratibida columnifera*)
Rocket Larkspur (*Delphinium ajacis*)
Scarlet Flax (*Linum grandiflorum rubrum*)
Siberian Wallflower (*Cheiranthus allionii*)
Sunflower (*Helianthus annuus*)
Sweet Alyssum (*Lobularia maritima*)

Heat Lovers

Amaranth (*Amaranthus hypochondriacus*)
Celosia (*Celosia spicata*)
French Lavender (*Lavandula stoechas*)
Persian Basil (*Ocimum basilicum*)
Salvia (*Salvia coccinea*)
Sunflower (*Helianthus annuus*)
Zinna (*Zinnia elegans, Z. angustifolia*)

Drought Tolerant

Annual Baby's Breath (*Gypsophilia elegans*)
Blanket Flower (*Gaillardia pulchella*)
Blue Flax (*Linum lewisii*)
California Poppy (*Eschscholzia californica*)
Purple Coneflower (*Echinacea purpurea*)
Rocky Mountain Penstemon (*Penstemon strictus*)
Wild Bergamot / Bee Balm (*Monarda fistulosa*)

(Partly) Shady Characters

Annual Baby's Breath (*Gypsophila elegans*)
Baby Blue Eyes (*Nemophila menziesii*)
Candytuft (*Iberis umbellate*)
Drummond Phlox (*Phlox drummondi*)
Forget-Me-Not (*Myosotis sylvatica*)
Foxglove (*Digitalis purpurea*)
Johnny-Jump-Up (*Viola tricolor*)
Lanceleaf Coreopsis (*Coreopsis lanceolate*)
Purple Coneflower (*Echinacea purpurea*)
Rocket Larkspur (*Delphinium ajacis*)
Sweet William Pinks (*Dianthus barbatus*)
Wild Columbine (*Aquilegia vulgaris*)

Herb Garden

Basil (*Ocimum basilicum*)
Bronze Fennel (*Foeniculum vulgare* 'Purpureum')
Chives (*Allium schoenoprasum*)
Dill (*Anethum graveolens*)
Italian Parsley (*Petroselinum crispum*)
Oregano (*Origanum vulgare*)
Rosemary (*Rosmarinus officinalis*)
Sage (*Salvia officinalis*)
Thyme (*Thymus vulgaris*)

Nature's Medicine

Calendula (*Calendula officinalis*)
English Lavender (*Lavandula angustifolia*)
Feverfew (*Tanacetum parthenium*)
German Chamomile (*Matricaria chamomilla*)
Oregano (*Origanum vulgare*)
Purple Coneflower (*Echinacea purpurea*)
Sage (*Salvia officinalis*)
Yarrow (*Achillea millefolium*)

Groundcover

Creeping Thyme (*Thymus serpyllum*)
English Daisy (*Bellis perennis*)
Faassens Catnip (*Nepeta faasenii*)
Johnny-Jump-Up (*Viola tricolor*)
Red Clover (*Trifolium pretense*)
Roman Chamomile (*Chamaemelum nobile*)

Seed Tape, Mats, and Disks

Seed tape, mats, and disks describe the different shapes of a seed planting tool where seeds are evenly spaced over biodegradable paper to make planting easier. They're a wonderful way to get ready for gardening before the season truly begins. They can be prepared in advance and stored so that when the soil is warm and ready for planting, you just roll out the seeds with perfect spacing every time.

How to Make Seed Tape

Materials
Toilet tissue
Flour
Water
Ruler
Paintbrush (fine tip)
Seeds

Make It!

1 Plan how long you want your seed tape to be. It could be in 12-inch (30-cm) strips that you can piece together in the garden or as long as your garden beds. Lay a strip of toilet tissue in your desired length. Fold the toilet paper in half lengthwise to mark the center point. Open the paper up again and lay it flat on a tabletop.

Mix equal parts flour and water to make a paste to affix the seeds to the paper.

2 Set a ruler on the center fold and use a paintbrush to dab dots of the flour-water paste in a line above the ruler, spacing the seeds as recommended on the seed packet. This line should approximately be in the middle of the top portion of the fold.

3 Place 1 seed on each dab of the flour-water paste. For very small seeds, dip the back end of the paintbrush into the paste and use it to pick up the seeds and attach them to the paper.

4 Use the paintbrush to apply the flour-water paste to the perimeter of one side of the paper, and then fold the two sides together.

5 Label the seed tape.

6 Allow the tape to dry completely and then wrap it around an empty toilet tissue roll for storage.

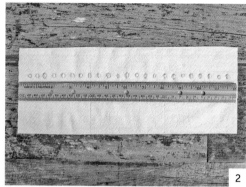

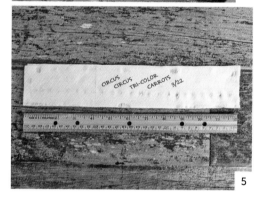

Seed Tape Recipes

Rainbow Carrots – mix heirloom red, yellow, orange, and purple carrots

Beets and Chard – alternate beets with chard on the seed tape

Lovely Lettuces – create a mesclun mix of leaf lettuces, arugula, and mustards in reds and greens

Zippy Zinnas – mix zinnia varieties by color, flower shape, and height

How to Make Seed Mats and Seed Disks

Making seed mats and disks is similar to making seed tape in different shapes. A seed mat in a rectangular or square shape can be useful for square foot planting and planning raised beds. Seed disks are round seed mats that are perfect for planting an instant container garden.

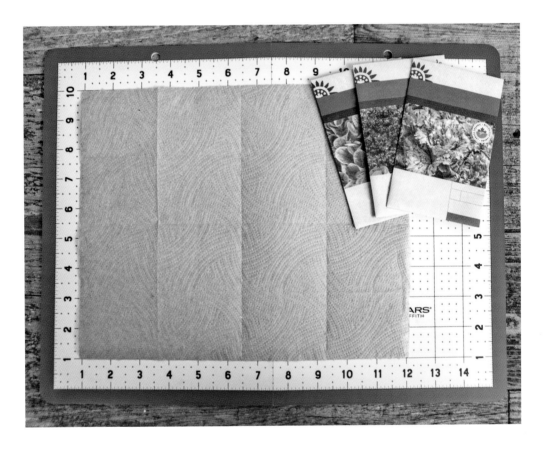

Materials

Unbleached paper dinner napkin or paper towel

Flour

Water

Paintbrush (fine tip)

Toothpick or bamboo skewer

Seeds

Make It!

1 Determine the dimensions and shape for your mats. Although each brand is different, a sheet or two of paper towel may be just the right dimensions for a square foot. A 6-inch (15-cm) four-fold napkin will unfold to a 12-inch (30-cm) square. A circle can be cut to fit inside a pot perfectly. There are so many options; simply prepare two pieces of paper in shapes you prefer.

2 Mix equal parts flour and water to make a paste to affix the seeds to the paper.

3 Lay a piece of paper on a flat surface and fold it to create a grid. Use a paintbrush to dab a bit of the flour-water paste where you want to plant the seeds, spacing them as recommended on the seed packet.

4 Place 1 seed on each dab of the flour-water paste. For very small seeds, dip the back end of the paintbrush into the paste and use it to pick up the seeds and attach them to the paper.

5 Use the paintbrush to apply the paste to the perimeter of the paper, and then place the second piece on top.

6 Label the paper.

7 Allow the mat or disk to dry completely and store until ready for planting.

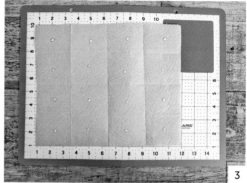

3

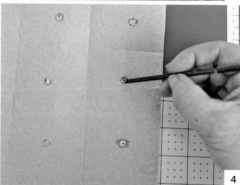

4

Seed Mat and Disk Recipes

Annual Herbs (mat) – mix parsley, sweet basil, purple basil, and borage

Beets and Radishes (mat) – alternate beets and radishes. When the radishes are harvested, it will make room for the beets.

Oh, Kale Yeah! (mat) – mix red and green kale varieties

Salad Bowl (disk) – mix lettuces, bitter greens, herbs, and chives

Presto Pesto (disk) – mix sweet and purple basil varieties

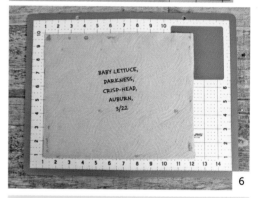

6

Planting Seed Tape, Mats, and Disks

Prepare the soil for planting and add the seed tape, mat, or disk on the soil. Cover with a fine 1-inch (2.5-cm) layer of soil and water well. Keep the top of the soil consistently moist through germination and as seedlings develop roots.

Chamomile Tea to Treat Damping Off

Damping off is a fungal disease that appears as a fuzzy, moldlike growth on plant stems and seeds, and on soil, usually with seedlings started indoors or in a greenhouse that has high humidity. To prevent fungal growth on seedlings, use German chamomile (*Matricaria chamomilla*) tea.

Materials

1 part fresh chamomile or one-fourth part dried

3 parts rainwater or dechlorinated water

2

Chamomile
Spray

3

1 There are two ways to make chamomile tea spray using either the fresh herb or the dried flowers. Only the flowers are used for making a flavored herbal tea for drinking, but you can include the leaves and stems for this recipe.

Fresh: Harvest fresh chamomile stems with leaves and flowers in the early morning when the flowers are at their peak of perfection. Make sun tea using fresh chamomile leaves and flowers in a Mason jar of water and set in the garden or on a sunny window to infuse for a day.

Dried: Brew a tea by pouring hot water over the dried flowers and letting it steep for 24 hours.

2 Strain the tea, cool, and use the mixture to water seedlings. Or add to a spray bottle to mist plants and the soil daily.

3 Chamomile tea can also be used as a foliar spray for preventing disease on established plants.

How to Dechlorinate Water

In many recipes in this book, water is noted as rainwater or dechlorinated water. Tap or garden water that comes from municipal sources is often treated with chlorine to remove and suppress microorganism growth. We want to encourage the growth of beneficial organisms as well as retain a plant's herbal properties. If you don't have a large enough supply of available rainwater, then allow water to sit in a wide-mouth bucket for 24 hours to allow the chlorine to evaporate or use boiled (and cooled) water.

Propagating Cuttings

Propagating cuttings is both an art and a science that is an easy and inexpensive way to multiply your stash of plants. There are a few different ways you can do it at home.

Rooting Cuttings in Water

Many houseplants, annuals, herbs, and vegetables with green, nonwoody stems can easily be rooted in water. Cut a 4- to 6-inch-long (10- to 15-cm-long) stem from the plant just below a bud using sharp, clean scissors or pruners. Strip off any lower leaves and flowers. Add the cutting to a glass of water and change the water daily for 3 to 4 weeks.

When roots grow to 1 to 2 inches (2.5 to 5 cm), transfer the cutting to transplant potting soil mix. Keep the soil watered but free-draining, and place the cuttings in a bright spot. Some plants also benefit from having the stem and leaves pruned to send more energy to the root development while creating a denser and bushier new plant.

Self-Watering Planter to Root Cuttings in Soil

Woody plants often root better in soil than in water, but it can be a challenge to keep the right amount of moisture. Too much water can rot the stem and new roots, while too little will dry up the stem. Never fear, a self-watering windowsill planter can easily be made with a plastic soda bottle.

Materials

Plastic soda bottle with cap

Scissors or box cutter

Hammer and nail

Cotton string

Transplant potting soil mix (see page 26)

Plant cutting

Clear plastic bag

Make It!

1 Cut a clean plastic soda bottle in half (into a top and bottom) using scissors or a box cutter.

2 Use the hammer and nail to poke a hole through the top of the cap.

3 Cut a 6-inch (15-cm) length of thick gauge cotton string. Thread the string through the hole and knot it on the inside of the cap.

4 Twist the cap back on the bottle.

5 Fill the bottom half of the bottle with water.

6 Invert the top of the bottle and fill with moistened transplant potting soil mix. Be sure that 2 inches (5 cm) of the string are inside the soil, leaving the 4 (10 cm) remaining inches hanging down.

7 Place the top of the bottle into the bottom of the bottle, so that the string is immersed in the water.

5

8 Cut a 4- to 6-inch-long (10- to 15-cm-long) stem from the plant just below a bud using sharp, clean scissors or pruners. Strip off any lower leaves and flowers. Place cuttings in the soil and check often to ensure that the soil remains damp but not soggy.

9 Place a plastic bag or cloche over the cuttings to create a mini greenhouse and keep the humidity levels up.

10 Transplant the cuttings to pots or the garden when they have strong roots that resist when you gently tug at the stem.

9

Willow Water Rooting Hormone Recipe

Willow (*Salix*) branches are rich with the hormone indolebutyric acid (IBA), which stimulates rooting, and salicylic acid (SA), which protects the cutting from fungi and bacterial infections. Make willow branch tea as a home-brewed rooting stimulator for propagating cuttings.

Materials

Young willow branches, the diameter of a pencil or smaller

Boiling water

Glass jar

Make It!

1 Harvest young branches of a willow tree, ideally first-year growth.

2 Remove and compost all of the leaves and cut the branches into 1-inch (2.5-cm) pieces.

3 Fill a jar half-full with branches and pour boiling water over the branches to fill the jar. Allow to steep overnight; strain the next day.

4 Soak new cuttings in willow water before rooting or use it to water cuttings. When rooting cuttings in water, dilute willow water to half-strength. Willow water can also be used to water seedlings. Store willow water in the refrigerator for up to 2 months.

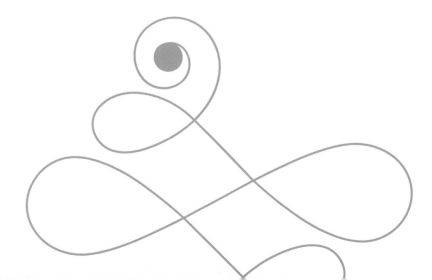

Compost

I'm often surprised when I learn someone doesn't compost because the process feels so natural to me. Then, when I see that same person buying compost for their garden, I'm gobsmacked! Even if you only have a small garden, composting is one of the most important activities you can do to save money and prevent waste from unnecessarily ending up in a landfill. Even more, it helps build far superior soil.

Have you ever looked closely at perfectly finished compost? Grab a handful and observe this rich, black, garden gold. It should have a uniform color, a light fluffy texture, and no strong smells. This material is the single most effective ingredient in creating a healthy garden.

Despite similar appearances, compost is not soil. Soil, as you remember from chapter 1, is made up of sand, silt, and clay particles. Compost is organic matter that has been broken down by soil microorganisms. It can be used as a soil amendment, fertilizer, and mulch,

all of which allow the organic matter to integrate with the native soil to improve its structure, moisture-holding properties, aeration, and nutrition.

Hooray for compost!

Composting isn't difficult, but it also isn't as simple as just throwing your kitchen scraps and garden cuttings into a heap and checking on them a year later. Eventually those items will break down and create compost, but there are much faster, cleaner, and more effective ways, which I will show in this chapter.

A Compost Recipe for Success

Healthy compost results from a combination of four ingredients: nitrogen, carbon, air, and moisture. It's important to note that more variety of materials going into the compost will mean more variety of the organisms and nutrients available in the completed compost.

The best way to keep your compost bin balanced is to ensure that no single nitrogen source exceeds more than 20 percent the volume of what you're adding.

1 PART NITROGEN SOURCE (GREENS)

Green compost ingredients are those with higher nitrogen content, such as grass clippings, garden trimmings, and kitchen scraps. These materials rot quickly and are full of the compounds needed for fast microbial growth. They are usually quite wet and heavy and can get stinky fast unless you balance them with enough brown material. When choosing greens for your compost bin, limit any one item to no more than 20 percent of the total of greens. This will help to mitigate any issues that could come up by packing the bin with so much of one item that it quickly throws the whole mix off.

2 TO 3 PARTS CARBON SOURCE (BROWNS)

Brown compost ingredients are those with higher carbon content, such as paper, finely shredded woody material, and straw. Browns are dry and bulky, creating spaces for air to reach the greens. They do not decay rapidly without greens because they do not hold enough moisture.

AIR

Oxygen is necessary for the microorganisms munching on the materials in the compost pile to turn it into compost. While you can certainly create a pile of greens and browns and let them do their thing, adding air to the pile stimulates the microorganisms into hyperdrive and will, therefore, speed up decomposition.

Introduce air by turning the compost with a fork, an aeration tool, or using a rolling composter. As the microbes work to break down the materials, the compost heap will become warm. The heat in the middle of the pile can reach up to 150°F (66°C) and then will cool down again after about 4 to 7 days. Turning the compost weekly helps stimulate the activity again, brings the temperature up, and moves the materials from the edges to the middle.

MOISTURE

Moisture is also necessary to give the microorganisms the best possible conditions to break down the material. After adding the materials, water the compost pile and mix it well. It should be damp but not soggy. In dry months you may have to add water, and in wet months you may have to protect the compost from rain.

Are Fallen Leaves "Browns?"

Color alone is not a good indication of what is considered brown materials. Deciduous leaves that have fallen and turned brown, as well as chopped tree and shrub clippings, have higher nitrogen balance than true "browns." Leaves and chopped-up clippings are excellent for compost and can decompose readily on their own, without a need for additional greens or browns. You can choose to compost these materials from the garden on their own or mix in with the 1 part green / 2 to 3 parts brown mixture. Just be sure not to replace all of the browns with fallen leaves or your compost will be too wet and stinky.

Keep These Materials Out of Compost

Not every material should go in your home compost bin, although some of these can go into city or county large-scale industrial compost bins where the temperatures are consistently hot enough to kill pathogens and seeds. Before you compost these items, be sure to check your local composting regulations.

• **Pesticides and herbicides** – Keep your garden healthy without introducing pesticides and herbicides into the compost bin.

• **Compostable grocery bags** – Despite their name, these should not go in your home compost bin. Use brown paper bags instead.

• **Evergreen clippings** – Some evergreens take a long time to compost at home and some resins can slow down and/or inhibit the composting process.

• **Meat, bones, dairy, or animal product food scraps** – Home compost doesn't get hot enough to break these down effectively, and it could attract pests.

• **Pet waste** – Dog and cat waste can carry pathogens that could be transferred to the soil.

• **Diseased plant material** – Diseased or infested plants may perpetuate the incidence of disease and pests in future years.

• **Plants that have gone to seed** – Compost may not get hot enough to sterilize seeds.

• **Large logs, thorny branches** – Big, woody items will be too large to break down. Chip or grind all large, woody materials instead.

• **Poison ivy, invasive weeds, and other noxious plants** – Don't risk spreading these plants by composting them.

COMPOSTING SHOULDN'T BE GROSS

If you think composting is yucky or dirty, you aren't doing it right! Compost should smell fresh, sweet, and earthy, like the forest. Overly stinky compost is not properly in balance, but it is an easy fix.

Too many greens, too much of one type of greens, or too much water in your compost could cause it to become soggy and smell bad. Compost can start to stink when there aren't enough carbon materials to balance out wetness. In this case, remove any of the soggy, offending materials, add more brown materials, and turn your compost to introduce air. In most cases, this will help remedy the problem.

Fruit Flies, Maggots, and Rats— Goodbye!

While healthy compost will contain beneficial bugs, bacteria, fungi, and other organisms, you shouldn't need to fight off an army of critters to get into the compost. Rodents love to burrow into a warm compost pile to create a nest while joining other wildlife like bears, raccoons, and fruit flies for a midnight snack. Designing your compost system to restrict access to wildlife is job one, but you can also eliminate the food source that is attracting them.

Insects will certainly be attracted to your compost pile and you want them there! Flies, maggots, beetles, and more can help the material to break down. If there is a particular insect species that is overly abundant and is becoming a nuisance (I'm looking at you, fruit flies), the best defense is removing the food source that is attracting them (likely fruit) and getting the compost pile back into balance. If you keep a layer of brown on the top of the compost to cover up the kitchen waste, it should keep the insects in check.

Choosing a Pile, Bin, or Other Composting System

How you set up your composting system depends largely on your available space. You can have one or as many compost areas as you need. The key is that they should be accessible and easy to add material to, aerate, and monitor its health. If you have a large property with different zones like a vegetable garden, agriculture space, a food forest, and/or managed woodland, you will want to add different composting systems for each one to provide an easy way to compost the waste from each zone and create enough to amend the soil. If you live in a small urban space, you may need to have a small closed system, a vermicompost bin, bokashi, or use a community composting program.

COMPOST SYSTEM	DESCRIPTION	BEST FOR
COMPOST PILE	A heap of materials left to compost in place	Large farmsteads, managed woodlands
SPOT COMPOSTING	Digging a hole in the soil and burying a mix of materials to compost below ground	Any garden
WOOD SLAT BIN	A compost bin with three sides made of wood slats	Areas without wildlife attracted to compost
CRITTER-PROOF BIN	A wood bin lined with 1/4-inch wire mesh on all sides as well as the top and bottom	Urban and suburban areas with rat, mice, raccoons, and other critters
ROLLING COMPOSTER	A closed system that doesn't sit directly on the soil. Compost turning is done by rolling the bin.	Urban areas and near homes where open bins can be unsightly
THREE-BIN SYSTEM	Three separate, side-by-side bins. One bin is for adding new material, another is left untouched to finish the compost, and a third is for finished compost available for use.	Large homesteads and farms
BEAR-PROOF BIN	Stone structure with metal top with holes for aeration	Bear country
ELECTRIC COMPOSTER	An expensive kitchen appliance that converts kitchen waste to compost in eight to twelve hours	Apartments
BOKASHI	Bokashi is a Japanese term for "fermented organic matter." Kitchen scraps are added to a bucket with bran and closed to ferment. After a few weeks, the fermented scraps are added to a compost system to finish.	Using in combination with another composting system
WORM BIN	A vermicomposting system that feeds worms kitchen waste and carbon material to produce worm castings	All gardens
COMMUNITY OR PUBLIC COMPOSTING PROGRAMS	Green waste collection from home or businesses, or community garden compost piles that allow compost sharing. The finished material is then also shared in the community.	Composters without space to compost

Compost Booster Recipe

Quick Return Composting is a method of accelerating composting developed by Maye Emily Bruce in the 1940s. In this method, a combination of plants is added to the compost pile to finish the compost in just 4 to 6 weeks. Traditionally, QR activator is made from six herbs: nettle, dandelion, chamomile, yarrow, valerian, and oak bark. The herbs are dried and then crushed into a powder. Honey and powdered milk are added to the powder to make a mix that is sprinkled on compost layers before adding a cover or insulation layer to the pile to hold in heat while maintaining airflow.

The intricacies of the QR method are featured in a book called *Quick Return Compost Making* by Andrew Davenport and Maya Emily Bruce. However, you can make a simple home garden compost activator with a custom blend of any combination of the following plants.

Compost Accelerating Plants

Alpine Strawberry
(*Fragaria vesca*)

Alfalfa (*Medicago sativa*)

Black Elderberry
(*Sambucus nigra*)

Calendula
(*Calendula officinalis*)

Chamomile
(*Matricaria chamomilla*)

Comfrey
(*Symphytum officinale*)

Dandelion
(*Taraxacum officinale*)

Hollyhock (*Althea rosea*)

Oak Bark (*Quercus robur*)

Sage (*Salvia officinalis*)

Stinging Nettle
(*Urtica dioica*)

Valerian
(*Valeriana officinalis*)

Yellow Dock
(*Rumex crispus*)

Just Add Plants

If you don't have the time or desire to grow, harvest, dry, and then grind the plants into compost accelerator, just toss some of the plants into the compost bin. Many gardeners grow comfrey—an exceptional compost booster—right beside the compost so they can simply cut off a bunch of leaves and stems and pop them right into the compost.

These Materials Speed Composting

Besides plants, manure and healthy soil are full of microbes, bacteria, fungi, soil insects, mites, and worms that will speed the decomposition process. Add a scoop of one or any combination of these compost amendments to really get the party started.

- Mushroom manure
- Well-rotted manure (not pet waste)
- Healthy garden soil
- Woodland soil from a healthy forest

Make It!

Grow compost accelerator plants in your garden or forage for wild plants from locations where foraging is permitted and safe. However, avoid harvesting plant parts that can easily reproduce, such as roots or seeds.

1 Hang bundles of freshly harvested plants from a rack in a cool, dry location until they are completely dried and can be crumbled in your hands.

2 Remove any hard or woody stems and bark and grind the dried plant material in a coffee grinder or blender reserved for making garden recipes. Cut the woody stems and bark into smaller pieces and use the coffee grinder to finely grind the pieces.

3 When all of the plants are reduced to a powder, mix them together and store them in sealed Mason jars labeled "Compost Booster" in a cool, dry place such as an indoor cabinet.

Use It!

If you are building a new compost pile, sprinkle the compost booster between layers as you build the pile. If you would like to accelerate decomposition of your existing compost, add ¼ to 1 cup (60 ml to 235 ml) of the compost booster in the center of the pile; turn the compost to mix it in.

DIY Vermicompost (Worm) Bin

Vermicomposting is the process of intentionally using worms to decompose kitchen scraps and carbon material resulting in worm castings (worm poop). Worm castings have a much finer texture than soil, are excellent at holding moisture, and are highly nutritious as a balanced garden fertilizer. While the N-P-K values will vary depending on what the worms have feasted on, worm poop is certainly rich with soil nutrients and microbes, making it a wonderful addition both to garden soil and compost. Above all, it's fun to make a worm bin and employ some worms who will happily take payment in kitchen scraps and pay you in poop.

Just like composting, vermicomposting requires these four ingredients: greens, browns, water, and air. The greens can be made up of kitchen scraps or garden waste, the browns provide bedding and shelter (and the worms also digest the bedding), the water they need typically comes from the provided kitchen waste, and the air comes from air holes that are added to the bins and the loosely packed material. Unlike composting, in vermicomposting, you add a fifth ingredient: worms.

The worms used in vermicomposting bins are not the earthworms you'll typically find in your garden. Specific varieties such as red wigglers (*Eisenia fetida*) and redworms (*Lumbricus rubellus*) are chosen because they are very active, and they love to spend their time eating and multiplying. When you create a worm bin and add a supply of worms, they will quickly get to work and start digesting the food and bedding material. They double their population each month to fill up the space that they've been given, but once the food supply or space becomes limited, they stop multiplying to control their own population. In most cases you won't have to worry about dividing or increasing your worms; they will manage that themselves. It's your job to give them a nice home, protection from the elements, and a whole lot of good food.

I have used a number of different bin designs, but my favorite is the personal design of Pau Farré, who teaches vermicomposting workshops at City Farmer in Vancouver, British Columbia. It is compact and easy to use, making it perfect for small urban composting, yet the design can be scaled to accommodate more worms and a large garden easily.

The bottom bin is used to collect the excess moisture (leachate), the middle bin is used to hold finished worm castings, and the top bin holds the worms plus their food and bedding.

Materials

2 nesting plastic bins, one with a lid

1 shallower bin in the same width

Power drill or hammer and nail

Four 2- to 3-foot-square wood blocks that can be used as risers

Dry material like shredded newspaper, straw, or dried leaves for bedding

½ lb, red wigglers (about 500 worms)

Kitchen scraps

Make It!

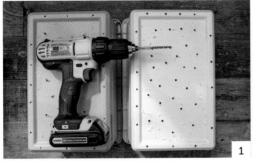

4 Add your worms to one corner.

5 Add about 4 cups (1 liter) of roughly chopped kitchen waste on top of the worms.

6 Cover with a top layer of dry bedding; any combination of straw, leaves, or shredded newspaper will do.

7 Assemble the worm bin. Place the 4 risers in the shallow bin to provide some clearance for the leachate to drain. If you plan to scale up to a larger bin, you may need to increase the number of risers to keep the base stable. Place the middle bin on them and add a bit of bedding inside that bin for the worms to explore.

8 Place the worm bin on top and add a lid.

9 Keep the vermicomposter outdoors in a cool, shady spot in summer, and a warm covered spot in winter. The temperature should be between 5° to 30°C (41° to 86°F). In areas that have cold winters, move the worms into a garage or, if it's not too cold, you can place a blanket over the top of the bin.

1 Drill drainage holes in the bottom of the two tall bins using a power drill or hammer and nail. **Note:** If the bins have uneven bottoms, drill holes in the lowest part of the bin to ensure that all the moisture drains out.

2 Make air holes on the sides of two upper bins using the same tools. The air holes should be spaced around the perimeter of the bin, above where the two bins overlap.

3 Fill one of the tall bins one-third full with a mixture of dry bedding materials as the base of your worm bin. Wet the bedding material so that it is the consistency of a wrung-out sponge.

Worm Food Recipe

Worms love to eat what you give them, but having a balance of different materials ensures the environment stays healthy. Just like composting, a good rule of thumb is to make sure that no more than 20 percent of their food is made up of one material.

Materials

Kitchen scraps, such as:

Raw vegetables

Egg shells

Coffee grounds

Flowers

Green leaves from garden

Avoid: cooked food, dairy, meat, bones, vinegar, oil, citrus, or juicy produce (e.g., tomatoes, watermelon)

Also, do not include any plant seeds, as worm digestion does not create the heat necessary to sterilize the seeds. (In fact, the seeds would be thrilled to germinate in nutrient-rich worm castings!)

Special dietary needs? You bet! Worms are raw-food, gluten-free vegans.

Make it!

1 Feed the worms weekly, alternating placing the food through the four corners of the bin. By the time a month has gone by, the worms will have had time to digest the scraps in the first corner.

2 The worms can easily survive for a month without food so don't worry if you need to go on vacation. Just feed them when you get home, and they will be happy to hold down the fort until you are back.

Troubleshooting

If the worm bin starts to smell, it's an indication that something has gone wrong. It should be fairly easy to detect by inspecting the four corners to see where the problem lies. Perhaps there were too many acidic foods in one area, which changed the pH to be off-putting to the worms. In this case, you will notice they have migrated as far away as possible and are hanging out where the conditions are more favorable. To fix the issue, clean out the material that's causing the problem, replace any affected bedding, and it should bring the bin back to health.

Worms Only, Please!

To prevent fruit flies, be sure that the bedding on top is dry and adequately covers the food. You can also omit the fruit or sweet scraps that attract flies. If neither of those things works, add a fruit fly trap (from chapter 5) nestled into the dry bedding at the top to attract them and drown them before they even get a taste of the kitchen scraps.

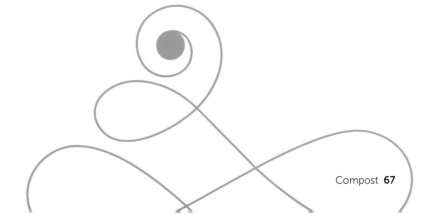

Harvesting Worm Castings

The bin is designed so the top bin contains the worms, bedding, and food, while the leachate falls through the holes into the bins below, settling in the catch tray at the bottom. The middle bin is for harvesting the castings.

Worm castings can be harvested every three to four months.

Use It!

To harvest the castings, stop feeding the worms for a few weeks until they have digested all of the kitchen scraps. Remove the dry top layer of bedding and swap the worms to be in place of the middle bin.

Set up the empty middle bin with new bedding and some kitchen scraps just as it was initially set up, but leave out the worms.

Put the freshly prepared bin on top of the one that contains the worms and castings and set the vermicomposter back in place. The worms will find their way up through the holes to get to the food.

When all the worms have finished digesting their food and migrated, you'll have a nice, clean supply of worm castings to use in the garden.

Dividing Worms

There may be a time when you would like to divide the population to give some worms away or start a second bin. To do this, remove the dry bedding top layer, then dump the remaining contents of the worm bin onto a tarp or tray and set it outside in bright light. The worms will migrate away from the light and huddle together. Gently scrape back the material until you reach the worms and quickly move them into their new home.

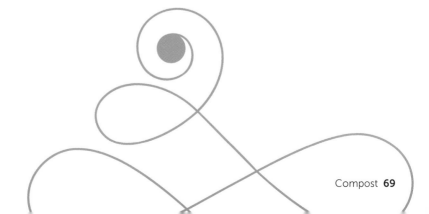

Compost Tea

Compost tea is a liquid made from steeping or brewing compost and water for the purpose of extracting beneficial organisms and water-soluble nutrients. Compost tea can be used as a soil drench, which applies dilute concentrations of soil microorganisms and nutrients to populate the soil. It can also be used as a foliar spray to add microorganisms to the aboveground plant parts, which can help with plant disease. Either way, compost tea is a beneficial way of extending the reach of compost to cover the garden.

For something that sounds so simple, compost tea is one of the most controversial topics in gardening and a difficult one to properly measure. Some experts say that watering with compost tea has no more benefits to the soil than plain water, while others swear by it as a staple for growing thriving crops. This variation in opinions makes sense considering that compost can be made of so many different inputs that it would be difficult to come to a standardized conclusion on its effectiveness. Even more, there are numerous methods for making compost tea that can yield additional variables.

The way around the debate is to give it a try and test the results in your own garden. As with all of the ideas in this book, you will learn what works best for your garden through observation and experimentation.

Common Sense and Safety with Compost Teas

Making compost teas is a simple process, but there is a potential for error when brewing microorganisms. You could end up increasing harmful organisms rather than beneficial ones. Here are some common-sense tips for working with compost tea:

- Start with an excellent quality finished compost. It should smell clean and fresh, not stinky, and it should be fully composted with little variation in the size or color of the particles.

- The water used should be either rainwater or dechlorinated water. Set an uncovered bucket of tap water out for 24 hours to allow the chlorine to evaporate.

- Do not use manure as an ingredient in compost tea.

- The resulting compost tea, whether it's an extract or an aerated brew, should also not have a strong odor. If the resulting tea smells like it has gone bad, it probably has. Do not use it in your garden.

- Use compost tea and extracts immediately when the brewing is complete. It should not be stored or set aside for later application.

- Test your homebrewed compost tea method on some container plants or one area of your garden that doesn't contain edible plants.

- Tea can also be sent for lab tests or inspected under a microscope.

- If you have any question about your ability to brew compost tea at home, search for a local workshop on making tea for personalized training suitable for you, your garden, and your geographical area.

Nature's Method: Topdress the Soil with Compost

The easiest and most natural way to feed your garden with compost tea is to allow Mother Nature to brew it for you. This method is particularly effective if you have a large amount of properly finished compost available to spread around your garden as you will need at least 1 to 2 inches (2.5 to 5 cm) of compost to topdress the soil. After that, cover the compost with 2 inches (5 cm) of mulch. This creates a protected layer of organic matter and microbes that will continue to break down and become part of the soil structure. Rain and garden watering will allow the compost tea to percolate down into the soil and allow the nutrients to be available to plants.

Grandmother Method: Compost Dilution

The first method of making liquid compost is the Grandmother Method, also called compost extract, anaerobic compost tea, or non-aerated compost tea. This is the common method of diluting compost passed down through generations.

It's similar to brewing yourself a cup of herbal tea. When you steep mint leaves or chamomile flowers in water, it infuses the water with the water-soluble nutrients that are more readily available for your body when they're sipped. To get those nutrients, you can certainly just eat the dried plant material, but it's not as gentle or as easy to absorb as a cup of tea. That said, you would get more fiber from eating the plant material, and that would help to fill up an empty stomach. This is an important connection to the garden because if you are using compost tea on your soil, it should have organic matter already present before you apply. Adding compost tea to depleted soil doesn't give the compost microorganisms anything to eat once they dive into the land.

Materials

1 part excellent quality finished compost

20 parts rainwater or dechlorinated water

Watering can or bucket

Make It!

Combine the compost and water in a watering can or bucket. Allow the compost to steep for 1 to 4 hours, stirring at least two to three times. When it's time to apply it to the garden, stir it well to mix the sediment in with the water. No need to strain out the compost that is left over; it can be watered into the soil with the liquid.

Alchemy Method: Aerated Compost Tea

In the Grandmother Method, I used the metaphor of steeping a cup of herbs as an example of how anaerobic compost tea is beneficial. Now, what do you think would happen if you left a cup of herbal tea steeping on the counter for a few days or a week? That's right, it would go bad. By "bad," I mean that after a day or so the warm tea and decomposing herbal tea create the perfect environment for bacteria to grow. If you left the tea on the counter like that for a week, I would not recommend drinking it!

The beneficial microbes in compost love air, while the bad bacteria typically enjoy stagnant, unaerated water.

In this system, air is continuously pumped into a bucket containing water and compost to brew more of the beneficial microbes. A compost tea brewer can be purchased as a kit or made at home using a 5-gallon (19 L) bucket, a nut milk bag, and an aquarium air pump. Visit https://gardentherapy.ca/compost-tea-brewer/ for the steps to make the brewer I use.

Materials

5-gallon (19 L) bucket compost tea brewer

Large 12- x 12-inch (30- x 30-cm) nut milk bag

1 cup (235 ml) excellent quality finished compost

1 cup (235 ml) worm castings

1 tablespoon (15 ml) soluble seaweed

Rainwater or dechlorinated water

Make It!

1 Add the water to the brewer and run the aeration for 1 hour.

2 Add the remaining ingredients to the filter bag and add to the water. Follow the instructions that accompany the brewer you are using.

3 Continue aerating for 24 hours at 72°F (22°C). If it is warmer, then decrease the brewing time, and if it is colder, increase the brewing time.

4 Strain the compost tea and apply to the garden immediately.

When cleaning up, thoroughly wash anything that was in contact with the organisms well to remove the biofilm and be ready for the next use.

Vermicompost Tea

Vermicompost tea is a liquid dilution of vermicompost with water. Dilute 1 part vermicompost with 10 parts water and let it sit for 1 to 12 hours. Use the dilution as a soil drench or foliar spray.

Leachate or Compost Tea

Leachate is the liquid that runs off compost and vermicompost bins as the compost materials break down. While most compost piles have direct contact with the ground soil, bin systems with closed bottoms need to have drainage holes and a catchment system for the liquid runoff.

This liquid is sometimes called compost tea; however, it is more accurately called leachate from the composting process. Compost tea is a dilution of finished compost, while leachate from compost or vermicompost bins consists of the excess moisture from the materials at all stages of composting. Fruit and vegetable juices can collect in the catchment as can rainwater. This is not necessarily the product of the microbial and chemical actions of composting; therefore, it can have very different properties. It could be made up of some finished compost runoff along with the excess liquid from that juicy watermelon you added to the bin.

Leachate can be strained using a fine-mesh strainer to remove any seeds that could still be viable. The leachate can be filtered from the catchment and added to the soil, although it's not clear what sort of benefit it could have considering it would be nearly impossible to tell what it contains.

Fertilizers and Garden Teas

Just as soil structure is essential to building a healthy garden, soil nutrition is equally important. Plants need a variety of nutrients to perform their best: primary nutrients (nitrogen, phosphorus, and potassium), secondary nutrients (sulfur, calcium, and magnesium), and a collection of micronutrients.

Plants growing in their native soil and conditions are able to extract the mix that they need from the soil and work within the ecosystem. Fallen plant material, soil wildlife, and companion plants create a cycle of resupplying nutrients back to the soil. In nature, fallen plant leaves decompose in place, building the soil and feeding the microorganisms. These plants may contain all that they need to feed the next year's growth, or they may have a symbiotic relationship with other plants.

In home gardens, we often disrupt the natural soil feeding systems that exist. We clean up spent plant material as opposed to letting it compost in place. The plants we grow may not be native to our area, or we may harvest parts of the plants that would continue its lifecycle such as flowers, fruit, and seeds. To have a lush and productive garden, nutrients need to replace that which we are removing and support the plants in growing the way they are meant to.

In most cases, adding an adequate amount of compost and organic mulch is enough to provide the nutrition plants need. There are times when a little extra nutrition can help boost fast-growing annuals, container gardens, indoor plants, and other types of gardens that do best with supplemental nutrition in the form of fertilizer.

Natural vs. Synthetic Fertilizers

Natural fertilizers are derived from minerals, plants, and animal products while synthetic fertilizers are synthesized chemicals of nutrients. While plants will use both natural and synthetic fertilizers indiscriminately, there are some important differences in how they function. Synthetic fertilizer molecules are made to be readily available to plants, and therefore can be hard to regulate. It's easy to overapply synthetic fertilizer and cause plants to take up too much nutrition, too quickly, causing fertilizer "burn." Additionally, leftover nutrients from synthetic fertilizers are washed away through the groundwater and can be a detriment to the ecological health of the surrounding areas and waterways.

Natural fertilizers are more forgiving because, often, they are not as readily available for plants. Soil wildlife such as bacteria, fungi, and insects break down the organic matter into plant-available forms. This supports the living biome of the soil, regulates the speed at which the nutrients are available, and encourages the plant to grow stable roots and expand the area that they collect nutrients from. Fertilizers from natural sources are a wonderful way to support plant growth while protecting soil life.

Primary Nutrients

Primary nutrients—N-P-K or nitrogen, phosphorus, and potassium—are required by plants in relatively large amounts. An imbalance of the primary nutrients can severely affect your ability to produce healthy plants.

Nitrogen: Nitrogen is the nutrient that stimulates plant growth above the soil. Nitrogen is also important in photosynthesis. An overabundance of nitrogen can cause plants to be tall and leafy, without producing flowers or fruit.

Phosphorus: Phosphorus stimulates root growth and flowering. It helps to establish young plants and aids photosynthesis, respiration, and growth.

Potassium: Potassium promotes all-around plant health, vigor, and disease resistance.

Secondary Nutrients

Secondary nutrients—sulfur, calcium, and magnesium—are also important to plants and are required in moderate amounts.

Calcium: Calcium is important for root and cell development and for ripening fruit and seed.

Magnesium: Magnesium helps plants absorb phosphorus, nitrogen, and sulfur. It also helps with seed ripening and germination.

Sulfur: Sulfur helps plants absorb calcium, magnesium, and potassium.

Micronutrients

Micronutrients are required by many plants and make up healthy soil. Trace elements such as iron, zinc, molybdenum, manganese, boron, copper, cobalt, silicon, and chlorine help plants grow heroically and fight off disease and pest threats.

Soil Amendments

Soil amendments are materials that can be added to the soil to amend its structure, pH, and available nutrients. Soil conditioners are an amendment that is primarily added to modify the soil structure to create space for air, water, and roots. Fertilizers primarily supply nutrients to support plant growth and feed the soil's microorganisms.

In many cases, organic amendments serve both as a soil conditioner and fertilizer. For instance, adding compost and mulch as a topdressing to gardens each year is a great way to continue to build healthy soil by adding organic materials that aerate the soil, hold on to moisture, and contain nutrients. If, however, after working to build the soil, your plants are not performing well or if there are excessive pest or disease problems, there are other natural materials that can be beneficial for the soil.

Observation, Experimentation, and Lab Testing

Whenever you read about soil amending and fertilizing, you will likely see a recommendation to do some soil testing first to determine what amendments you may need to add. There are home tests available that can evaluate the N-P-K levels in your soil and lab tests that can monitor a few more factors as well.

For a healthy home garden, soil lab tests are often not a worthwhile expense. In most cases, soil testing covers only pH, soil structure, and some nutrients levels. Most of this can be approximated through the DIY tests from chapter 1 in addition to observation and experimentation.

If you have any concerns about toxicity in the soil, like heavy metals, pesticides, and herbicides, it's certainly worth finding a testing facility that can perform a thorough evaluation of your soil health and provide recommendations how to repair it.

The bottom line: Unless you are farming agricultural land or have serious health issues with your soil, following the recipes and ideas in this book will allow you to build garden health over the long term while giving you the skills to learn what works and what doesn't in your space.

COMPOST

Adding garden compost to your garden beds is a free and environmentally friendly way to improve the organic matter, microbes, and soil structure. Regularly add properly finished and screened compost to garden beds as it is ready throughout the year.

LIME

Garden lime is ground limestone rock, which is a slow-release amendment for treating acidic soil. It contains calcium carbonate, so it not only raises the soil pH, but it also adds calcium. Dolomite lime contains magnesium as well.

ROCK PHOSPHATE

This is a slow-release mineralized source of phosphorus for amending soil. Most home gardens have adequate amounts of phosphorus in the soil and therefore rock phosphate is not needed. (See the sidebar "Phosphorus in the Home Garden.")

MINERAL ROCK DUST

Mineral rock dust has many other names such as glacial rock dust, soil remineralizer, and mineral fines. It is a slow-release, finely crushed rock that contains secondary nutrients (magnesium, iron, and manganese) and trace elements. Rock dust helps remineralize the soil and improves soil structure, moisture retention, and drainage.

GREENSAND

Greensand is a shallow marine mineral that is mined. It provides iron, potassium, magnesium, and manganese. Greensand also helps improve the soil structure by loosening hard, compacted soil while also improving its moisture- and nutrient-retention properties. Greensand is quite versatile as a soil amendment. It can absorb excess water in clay soils and hold water for plant availability in sandy soils.

BONE MEAL

Bone meal is finely ground bovine, poultry, or fish bones that provide a high level of phosphorus. There is a long-standing recommendation that bone meal should be added to the planting hole of new shrubs and trees, but additional phosphorus is not needed in most home garden soils. (See the sidebar "Phosphorus in the Home Garden," on page xx.)

BLOOD MEAL

Blood meal is a byproduct of cattle and hog farming that is very high in nitrogen and full of trace minerals. It comes in a dried powder form and can be included in certified organic soil mixes (although this doesn't necessarily mean that the animal or farm was certified organic). Alfalfa meal is a plant-based alternative to blood meal.

ALFALFA MEAL

Alfalfa meal is a source of nitrogen and potassium plus a broad spectrum of other minerals, vitamins, amino acids, and the growth hormone triacontanol. It helps improve the soil structure and helps plants access nutrients. Alfalfa meal is also a great amendment to activate the compost pile.

KELP MEAL

Kelp meal has low levels of nitrogen and potassium, but it is used more as a soil amendment due to its multitude of readily available trace elements and over 60 naturally chelated minerals. Kelp meal also improves soil structure, prevents nutrient leaching, and increases soil's water-holding capacity. The benefits of kelp meal can aid the soil for many years after its application.

WOOD ASH

Wood ashes can be added to garden soil to raise soil pH, and they are also a source of potassium, calcium, and magnesium. Note that wood ash can cause salt injury, so it's best to use less than one would use lime in the garden.

BIOCHAR

Biochar is the charcoal left over from burning lumber waste or other organic material at a very high temperature in a low-oxygen environment, which is called "pyrolysis." The resulting material is pure carbon, which is exceptional at holding nutrients and moisture in the soil. Raw biochar needs to be inoculated, or "charged," with nutrients or it will absorb nutrients from the soil. Combine raw biochar with compost and compost tea or worm castings and leachate for one month to inoculate it before adding to soil. Alternatively, add biochar directly to your compost pile and it will be added to the garden when the compost is finished.

OYSTER SHELL FLOUR

Oyster shell flour is another name for finely ground oyster shells, which consist of approximately 95 percent calcium carbonate and many minerals. It supports root development, raises the pH in acidic soils, and aids plants with nutrient absorption. It's beneficial when added to soil where one plans to grow tomatoes, cucumbers, zucchini, and other vegetables that succumb to blossom end rot, which is a sign of calcium deficiency that results from inconsistent irrigation.

WORM CASTINGS

Worm castings are worm-digested organic material—a.k.a., vermicompost. They are nutrient-rich and contain many microbes. Worm castings retain soil nutrients and moisture allowing both to be more available for plant uptake. Worms filter out heavy metals and contaminants from the soil, which makes castings an excellent fertilizer for organic gardens.

COFFEE CHAFF

Coffee chaff is the light and papery outer husks of coffee beans that are removed when the beans are roasted. Coffee roasters produce an abundance of chaff as a waste product and are often happy to give it away to eager gardeners. Coffee chaff is rich in nutrients and has an oily or waxy consistency, so it is best added in moderation to the compost bin rather than directly to the soil.

MYCORRHIZAE

Mycorrhizae are beneficial fungi that live in the soil. Visit a forest and gently pull back the humus layer on top to see the white, weblike networks of mycorrhizae that help plant roots draw nutrients, stimulating plant growth and root development. When garden soil is disturbed through digging or turning, the mycorrhizal network is destroyed. Many bagged soil mixes can be found that contain these beneficial fungi; however, there is a question as to whether or not they can live in a bagged product and be transferred successfully to the garden. The best way to add mycorrhizae to a garden is to create a hospitable environment for them to grow as they do in the forest. Layer compost and mulch on the top of the soil and leave the soil structure below undisturbed.

ANIMAL MANURES

Organic animal manures are inexpensive soil amendments, but they vary widely in nutrient content depending on the type of manure and its age. Fresh animal manures that have not been composted with bedding (like straw) have higher nutrients. As manure ages and is exposed to rain, its nutrition levels drop. Manure should be composted at high temperatures to kill any pathogens that can be transferred to the soil and root vegetables. Be sure to look for manure from local organic farms to ensure that you are not adding unwanted medications, pesticides, and herbicides to your garden.

MUSHROOM MANURE

Mushroom manure is a byproduct of mushroom farming. It is usually made up of the composted substrate medium used to grow mushrooms. This substrate can contain a wide variety of ingredients, such as animal manure, animal bedding, wood chips, peat moss, gypsum, blood meal, soybean meal, potash, lime, and chalk. Look for organic mushroom manure as a soil amendment for garden beds. Use this rich manure sparingly or allow well-composted manure to sit uncovered from fall to spring before adding it to the garden to avoid salt injury.

N-P-K of Animal Manures

SOURCE OF MANURE	N-P-K*	BENEFITS	WARNINGS
CHICKEN	3-2-2	Very high in nitrogen. Weed seeds destroyed when digested.	Must be composted. Too strong for direct application.
COW/STEER	1.3-2-2 08-0.5-0.5	Easily composted.	
HORSE	0.5-0.2-0.6	Rich in organic matter. Often includes straw.	Can be filled with undigested herbicides like Clopyralid and Aminopyralid that will harm plants. Use caution.
SHEEP/LLAMA	0.4-0.3-0.8	Well digested and high in potassium.	Labor-intensive to collect manure from field grazers.
RABBIT	2-1.4-0.6	High in nitrogen and phosphorus.	
MUSHROOM	0.7-0.3-0.3		Usually still contains animal byproducts in its composted substrate.

N-P-K can vary widely from these numbers as it depends on the source, animal feed, and composting methods. Ask for data from the supplier for the most accurate numbers.

Phosphorus in the Home Garden

Rose and bulb fertilizers are often labeled as "bloom boosters" because the high levels of phosphorus encourage flowering in plants. If you're noticing that your container plants and hanging baskets aren't flowering as much as they should be, then adding some additional phosphorus could be the key to more blooms. That being said, the ground soil in a home garden probably has adequate amounts of phosphorus. Adding more than is needed by the plants can run off into water systems, which creates environmental issues. Even more concerning is that phosphorus is a finite resource and humans are consuming it for agriculture purposes at alarming rates. While farmed land may need phosphorus to be replenished, in the home garden it is only needed when a soil test shows a deficiency or when fertilizing plants in potting soil.

WHEN TO AMEND?

As organic amendments are much slower to release nutrients into the soil, amend gardens in fall for spring planting to give the amendments time to become available to plants. The exception is composted manures, as many of the nutrients are already soluble and ready for plant uptake.

Fertilizer Recipes

There are many pre-blended fertilizer mixes available to purchase commercially, but it can be much more economical (and satisfying) to create your own blend of organic fertilizer.

GRANULAR NATURAL FERTILIZER BLENDING

Many natural fertilizers are sold in granular form. The packaging will list its N-P-K analysis and possibly list any other secondary nutrients and micronutrients it contains. Granular natural fertilizers are easy to use, forgiving to blend, and release nutrients slowly in the soil. Even better, the dry granules can be mixed together to create fertilizer blends to best support the types of plants you are growing.

The key to making your own dry organic fertilizer blends is to create variety in your blend so that there are different types of available N-P-K as well as sources for secondary nutrients and micronutrients.

Fertilizing Sick Plants

Fertilizers are intended to enhance the production of your garden, not solve plant health issues. Plants can be sick for many reasons, and if you are adding organic matter and supporting healthy soil, then soil fertility is not likely to be the issue. Plant health issues are best looked at individually and tested to look for solutions. Air temperature, soil temperature, overwatering, underwatering, herbicides, pesticides, plastics, diseases, fungi, pests, and soil toxicity are just some of the reasons that plant health can fail. Fertilizing won't help in those cases.

Creating your own dry fertilizer blends is meant to be used as a plant booster that works along with the other components of this book, such as building healthy soil with compost and mulching.

If you have specific nutrient deficiencies they will show up as plant health indicators such as disease, pests, dieback, and discoloration. If your plants are not performing well, and you think that it might be a nutrient deficiency, there are some things you can try:

- Revisit soil health, structure, and pH.
- Try adding a balanced fertilizer blend.
- Send away soil for a lab test (although keep in mind that some nutrients are not evaluated in soil tests).
- Contact your local Master Gardeners Extension Service for advice.
- Remove the plant and try a different plant in its place.

Fertilizers and Water Solubility

While it seems that you could simply add the granules to a gallon (3.8 L) of water to extract the nutrients, it's not that simple. The nutrients must be water-soluble to be converted from a dry application to a liquid form. As we discussed earlier, many organic fertilizers work because microbes need to consume and digest them to make the nutrients available to plants. For many of the dry ingredients, it is not possible to make a liquid fertilizer by dissolving it in water. There are a few that are at least partially water-soluble, though, and they make a lovely liquid fertilizers, like the recipe for "Indoor Plant Fertilizer," on page 96.

GRANULAR FERTILIZER BLEND INGREDIENTS

There are many organic sources for dry granules that can be used as fertilizer. Some are easier to find than others; some are byproducts of animal farming; and some come from fishing, mining, and farming. In any case, it's worth a bit of time looking at each one of the sources that's available to you and evaluating whether or not it's something that you want to use to fertilize your plants.

These are also the ingredients that make up many commercial organic blends. They can be certified as "organic" because the material is organic (in that it comes from nature), but it doesn't necessarily mean that the materials come from certified organic farms. The source for each product varies widely and can have quite different N-P-K ratings. The following lists some examples of N-P-K on products available in North America.

NITROGEN SOURCES	N-P-K	AVAILABILITY	NOTES
BLOOD MEAL	14-0-0	fast	repels deer
FEATHER MEAL	13-0-0	slow	
FISH MEAL	9-4.5-0	moderate	odor can attract pests
SOYBEAN MEAL	7-1-2	slow to moderate	one of the largest GMO crops
SHRIMP MEAL	6-6-0	slow	source of calcium and chitin*
COTTONSEED MEAL	5-2-1	slow	acidic
ALFALFA MEAL	3-0-3	slow	growth hormone triacontanol
CRAB MEAL	4-3-0	slow	source of calcium and chitin*
PHOSPHORUS SOURCES			
ROCK PHOSPHATE	0-3-0	slow	
SOFT ROCK PHOSPHATE (SOLUBLE)	0-5-0	slow	
MINERALIZED PHOSPHATE	0-13-1	slow	finite resource
BONE MEAL	2-16-0	slow to moderate	
FISHBONE MEAL	6-18-0	fast	
NEEM SEED MEAL	6-2-1	slow	also called Neem cake
POTASSIUM SOURCES			
MINED POTASSIUM SULFATE/POTASH	0-0-50	very fast	very water soluble, doesn't add bulk to the soil
KELP MEAL	1-0.5-3	fast	
WOOD ASH	0-1-3	fast	can cause salt injury, use with caution
ALFALFA MEAL	3-0-3	slow	
LANGBEINITE	0-0-22	moderate	
GREENSAND	0-0-3	very slow	
SEAWEED	1-1-17	fast	

*Chitin helps with plant immunity and nematode control.

All-Purpose Blend 7-7-7

Adding an all-purpose fertilizer can increase vegetable and flower production. Apply in early spring before planting.

- 3 parts blood meal
- 3 parts bone meal
- 1 part potassium sulfate

Easy Peasy Two-Ingredient Blend 2.8-3.2-2.4

Just two ingredients make up this fertilizer blend.

- 4 parts alfalfa meal
- 1 part bone meal

Plant-Based Recipe 3-1-2

This recipe has no animal products or mined minerals.

- 3 parts kelp meal
- 2 parts alfalfa meal
- 2 parts Neem seed meal
- 1 part cottonseed meal

Land and Sea Recipe 5-5-5

Nutrients from the sea make up the majority of this blend, with some mined minerals to balance it out.

- 2 parts fish meal
- 1 part fishbone meal
- 1 part kelp meal
- 1 part langbeinite

Annual Flower Boost 2.8-6.0-1.4

Adding fertilizers can increase both flower size, number of blooms, and keep blooms lasting longer.

- 3 parts shrimp meal
- 3 parts bone meal
- 2 parts alfalfa meal
- 2 parts greensand
- 1 part kelp meal

Container Garden Fertilizer 4-3-2

This container garden fertilizer includes fast-acting fertilizer for strong performance in a short growing season.

- 4 parts kelp meal
- 1 part fishbone meal
- 1 part blood meal

APPLICATION RATE

"Home gardeners tend to over-fertilize flower and vegetable beds. Plan to reduce or eliminate fertilizer applications in these areas if an inch or more of organic matter is incorporated into the soil of established beds at least once a year."
—University of Maryland Extension

The only true way to determine how much fertilizer your garden needs is to get a soil lab test done that will report how much fertilizer is needed. In the absence of a soil test, look to the application rates on the ingredients you are blending, and use those as your guideline, using the least amount suggested to start. Knowing that fertilizer is a supplemental source of nutrients, it is not necessary to have a heavy hand. Applying small amounts of fertilizer at regular intervals will allow you to judge the effectiveness and adjust your application depending on the results.

Texas A&M University System AgriLife Extension recommends using 2 to 3 pounds (0.9 to 1.4 kg) of fertilizer, such as 10-20-10 for every 100 square feet (9.3 square meters) of garden area. Use 2 pounds (0.9 kg) of fertilizer if the garden is sandy and 3 pounds (1.4 kg) if the soil is mostly clay." *Editor's note: Metric measurements added by publisher.*

That being said, there are a few general guidelines for different garden formats like raised beds, container gardens, and indoor plants.

GARDEN BEDS	2 lbs. per 100 sq. ft. (.9 kg per 9 sq. meters); determine needs based on soil test
RAISED BEDS (VEGETABLES)	¼ cup per square foot (59 ml per .09 square meter)
CONTAINERS / HANGING BASKETS	1 Tbsp. per gallon (15 ml per 3.8 liter)

Save the Epsom Salts for Your Bath

The internet is filled with the magical powers of Epsom salts for your garden as a fertilizer and miracle cure from everything from pest problems to leaf diseases. But does your garden really need it? Likely not. Epsom salts are magnesium sulfate, and while magnesium and sulfur are secondary nutrients essential for plant health, they are rarely deficient in the home garden. If you are building healthy soil with compost and organic matter, there is surely more than enough of these nutrients for your plants. Epsom salts are much better used in your bathtub, where they can give your sore muscles some pampering after a day out tending to the garden.

Garden Teas and Foliar Sprays

Garden teas are home-brewed liquid fertilizer preparations that extract soluble nutrients to be spread back into the garden through the soil or through direct application to a plant's leaves. Liquid fertilizers can be used as a soil drench applied to the soil when watering or as a foliar spray. Garden teas and foliar sprays should be used with caution and should be highly diluted to avoid injuring plants.

Green Garden Tea

Green garden tea is a great way to use garden and lawn trimmings to quickly add nutrients into water for the garden. Making garden tea is as simple as making tea, although in much larger batches.

Materials
Two 5-gallon (19 L) buckets, one with a lid

Drill

Lawn and garden clippings

Rainwater or dechlorinated water

Make It!

1 Drill holes in the bottom of one of the buckets to make a strainer. Set the bucket with holes inside the second bucket.

2 Collect garden clippings that are green, healthy, and full of nitrogen, like freshly mowed grass clippings from lawns free of chemical herbicide or fertilizer. Avoid any diseased, pest-infested plant material or seeds, as this process will not sterilize the plants.

3 Roughly chop the clippings by making a pile and cutting into it using hedge shears or running over them with a lawnmower. Pack the clippings into the nesting buckets two-thirds of the way full; submerge the clippings in rainwater. Stir to allow the water to saturate the entire contents of the bucket.

4 Put the lid on the top bucket and leave it in the garden for three days. Stir at least twice each day.

5 Strain the garden tea from the water by lifting the top bucket and allowing the water to drain through to the bottom bucket.

6 Dilute 1 part garden tea with 10 parts rainwater when watering the garden.

1

4

Making Foliar Spray

Make a garden tea into a foliar spray by diluting the mixture as directed in the recipe and straining it through fine fabric like cheesecloth, a nut milk bag, or a pillowcase. Add the liquid into a spray bottle and add a few drops of Castille soap to help it stick to the foliage. Apply the spray to leaves in the morning before the heat of day. Always test on one leaf/plant before widespread application.

Weed Tea

Weed tea is made a little differently than green garden tea, as the material is filtered through fabric to ensure that no weed seeds or plant parts are reintroduced into the soil.

Materials

One 5-gallon (19 L) bucket with lid

Cotton pillowcase

Drill

Rainwater or dechlorinated water

Weeds and wild plants

PLANT	NITROGEN (N)	PHOSPHORUS (P)	POTASSIUM (K)	CALCIUM (CA)	SULPHUR (S)	MAGNESIUM (MG)	MICRONUTRIENTS*
ALFALFA	x						Fe
BENTGRASS (*Agrostis* SPP.)					x		Mn, Cu, Zn
BORAGE (*Borago officinalis*)				x			
BINDWEED (*Convolvulus arvensis*)		x	x	x			
CHAMOMILE (*Matricaria chamomilla*)		x	x	x			
CHICKWEED (*Stellaria media*)		x	x				
CLOVER (*Trifolium* SPP.)	x	x					
COMFREY (*Symphytum officinale*)	x		x	x		x	Fe
DANDELION (*Taraxacum officinale*)		x	x	x		x	Fe, Cu, Si
DOCK (*Rumex obtusifolias*)		x	x	x			Fe
FENNEL (*Foeniculum vulgare*)	x	x					
GARLIC (*Allium sativum*)					x		
KELP (*Laminaria digitate*)	x			x	x	x	
LAMB'S QUARTERS (*Chenopodium album*)	x	x	x	x			Mn
LUPINE (*Lupinus* SPP.)	x	x					
MULLEIN (*Verbascum* SPP.)			x		x	x	Fe
OAK BARK (*Quercus robur*)			x				
PIGWEED / REDROOT (*Amaranthus retroflexus*)		x	x	x			Fe
PLANTAIN (*Plantago major*)					x		Mn, Fe
PURSLANE (*Portulaca oleracea*)			x	x	x	x	Mn
STINGING NETTLE (*Urtica dioica*)	x		x	x		x	Fe, Cu
VALERIAN (*Valeriana officinalis*)							Si
YARROW (*Achillea millefolium*)	x	x	x			x	Cu

*Micronutrients: Manganese (Mn), Iron (Fe), Copper (Cu), Cobalt (Co), Zinc (Zn), Silicon (Si)

2

Make It!

1 Finely chop the weeds using hedge shears, a lawnmower, or a leaf blower on reverse. Be careful when using electric tools like a lawnmower because rocks, roots, and twigs can fly out or damage the equipment.

2 Add the weeds to a pillowcase and set it inside a 5-gallon (19 L) bucket. Pour rainwater over the clippings to completely cover.

3 Put a lid on the bucket and leave it in the garden for 3 days; stir at least twice each day.

4 Strain the garden tea from the water by lifting the pillowcase and pressing out the water.

5 Dilute 1 part weed tea with 10 parts rainwater when watering the garden.

Comfrey Garden Smoothie

Technically, this concoction is a slurry, but the gorgeous green deliciousness looks and smells so good I've renamed it a garden smoothie. They both refer to the same thing, blending a solid food with a liquid to make a thicker liquid that easily delivers nutrients. In a smoothie, it's typically fruit and vegetables blended into a delicious drink, and this comfrey smoothie is no different, except you don't drink it. Instead, you serve it to your plants. Comfrey is glorious food for your garden and pureeing it in a blender is a great way to spread the goodness throughout the garden while watering.

The same reason comfrey is so prolific in the garden is the reason why it makes a good fertilizer. Comfrey is a vigorous grower in any soil because it has a taproot that reaches deep and is very effective at drawing up hard-to-access nutrients from the soil. When those big leaves are chopped, blended, and added to water, they will quickly send nutrients back to the soil.

Materials

1 part comfrey leaves

3 parts rainwater or dechlorinated water

Blender

Watering can

Make It!

Cut up the comfrey leaves and add them to a blender. Fill the blender with water and purèe the leaves into a slurry. Use immediately, 1 tablespoon (15 ml) per gallon (3.8 L) when watering; discard any leftovers into the compost bin.

Miracle Plant or Invasive Weed?

If you grow comfrey, then you are either a huge fan of this super herb or you think I'm completely off my rocker for suggesting it be included in the home garden. Comfrey—and many other medicinal wild plants like dandelions and stinging nettle—is so prolific in the garden that oftentimes a gardener is cursing these as horrid weeds rather than praising their tenacity. Yet that is exactly *why* we should be praising them. Their deep taproots that are nearly impossible to dig up will break up hard, compacted soil and mine deep down for vital minerals. The soil loosens, and the plants then drop their leaves full of nutrition to compost in place and rebuild the soil.

Amazing, right?

And just to make sure there are plenty of these plants to do the hard work of repairing the soil, they set a gazillion seeds and plant themselves everywhere. In the 1950s a sterile comfrey variety called 'Bocking 14' was developed for gardeners who wanted to include this lovely plant without it taking over the entire garden. If you have ever tried to dig one up, you know that even the tiniest part of the root will grow back into a robust leafy giant in just a few months. If you want to include comfrey, but fear the repercussions, you have a safer option by planting 'Bocking 14'. For everyone else, plant comfrey, harvest it liberally, and reap the benefits.

Indoor Plant Fertilizer 5-2-5 (Undiluted)

There are times when it's easier to use a liquid fertilizer than a granular one, such as when you are watering houseplants. In summer, houseplants respond to warmth and light, and it stimulates their growth. But due to the closed system of soil they live in, they are completely dependent on their human plant parents for available nutrients.

It's good practice to add a slow-release dry fertilizer at planting and again annually. In summer, plants will benefit from an application of an additional water-soluble fertilizer. And you will appreciate having one that doesn't have a strong odor! Many homebrew liquid fertilizers are filled with microorganisms that support healthy outdoor soil but are not great for indoor soil.

Materials

1 tablespoon (15 ml) soluble seaweed

1 tablespoon (15 ml) alfalfa meal

1 tablespoon (15 ml) blood meal

1 tablespoon (15 ml) soft rock phosphate

1 gallon (3.8 L) rainwater or dechlorinated water

Make It!

1 Measure the ingredients and add them to a glass bottle or jar with a lid. Stir well to combine and shake well before each use.

2 Dilute the fertilizer by adding ½ cup (120 ml) of the liquid fertilizer blend into 4 cups (950 ml) of water in a watering can. Water houseplants with the diluted fertilizer mix monthly in spring and summer and discontinue use in fall and winter.

Use the diluted fertilizer immediately. The prepared fertilizer can be stored in a cool, dark location for up to 3 months. Discard if the liquid shows signs of spoilage such as discoloration, mold, or an unpleasant odor.

Alfalfa Tea for Seedlings and Roses

Alfalfa is prized as a cover crop and as a fertilizer for its high levels of nitrogen. It is also rich with vitamins (A, D, B1, B6, E, K, and U) and minerals (calcium, iron, magnesium, phosphorus, and zinc) and also contains the growth hormone triacontanol. This growth hormone makes alfalfa tea a great fertilizer for seedlings when applied after they have developed their first two true leaves. The American Rose Society also sings its praises and recommends feeding homebrewed alfalfa tea to roses and perennials.

Materials

½ cup (120 ml) alfalfa meal

1 gallon (3.8 L) rainwater or dechlorinated water

Make It!

You can easily adjust the volume of this recipe for your garden needs. For a smaller amount to feed seedlings, add the ingredients to a large, glass Mason jar with a lid and infuse in a warm place in direct sunlight. For a larger amount to feed roses and perennials, add the ingredients to a 5-gallon (19 L) bucket or large bin.

1 Measure the ingredients and add them to the container of your choice.

Stir well, cover with a lid, and set in the sun. For best results brew for at least 36 hours, stirring at least twice each day. The brew is ready when the solid material settles at the bottom and the liquid above is an orange color. It should smell sweet and fresh, like hay.

2 To apply, move the tea out of the sun to cool, and then stir the ingredients again. Pour the tea directly from the jar or bucket onto your plants, being careful not to displace soil and roots. Strain the mixture through a pillowcase if you prefer to add it to a watering can.

Birds, Bees, and Bugs

Gardens and insects go together like bees and honey. If you want honey, you need bees. And if you want a thriving organic garden, you need insects. While there are many available books where you can look up "good" bugs and "bad" bugs, it's not quite as black and white in as it sounds. Ants may be farming aphids on your rose bushes, but they are also working hard in the garden to clean up debris and aerate the soil. That pretty white butterfly pollinating your garden is the mature form of the very same cabbageworm that decimated your cabbage, kale, and mustards.

Even if you can determine the bugs you want from those you don't, a few pests are expected and even beneficial to your garden. Without some pests, what would the beneficial insects have to eat? If beneficial insects get too hungry, they will move on to search for food elsewhere, or, worse, die. Allowing small populations of pests in your garden creates a more balanced ecosystem. It's when pest populations get out of control that you need to step in.

If you have implemented the ideas in this book so far, you are well on your way to creating a regenerative, self-maintaining garden. Healthy soil and robust plants will be able to tolerate pest populations without too much damage. The organic plants you are growing and the mulch layer on the soil create the ideal habitat for natural predators and pollinators. Supporting those critters by providing food, water, breeding areas, and winter shelter help support the health of your garden space. In this chapter, we will take a look at recipes to support beneficial wildlife and some of the traps and deterrents for pests.

Butterfly Puddler

Butterflies, moths, and even leaf-hoppers enjoy having a little mud puddle in the garden. This doesn't have to be a large area or a complicated structure; simply a spot for them to suck up some muddy water for a refreshing drink of minerals. Be sure to place the puddler in a sunny location that is easily visible from your home or garden. You definitely won't want to miss the fun from watching the show.

Materials

Terracotta pot and plant tray

Play sand

Compost

Decorative rocks and beach glass

Make It!

1 Mix 3 parts sand with 1 part compost and add it to the tray of the terracotta pot.

2 Make a "river" in the sand by pushing aside some of the sand and adding decorative pebbles.

3 Lay flat decorative rocks or beach glass along the river. These perches sit just above the sand and compost and give butterflies and friends a place to land. The pattern you choose to lay out the rocks is purely for your design pleasure.

4 Add some water to the sand and compost to make mud and set the puddler out in the garden.

Fill the water every few days to a week depending on the weather and how quickly the water evaporates. Each month, empty the puddler and give it a good wash with biodegradable dish soap. Also refresh the sand, compost, and design.

1

2

3

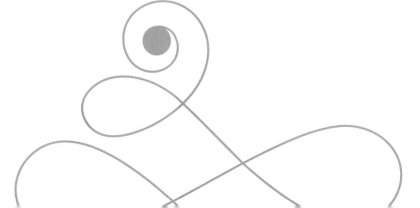

Bee Bath

Creating a bee-friendly garden means more than just planting flowers. You certainly want to attract them with gorgeous blooms, but while they are in your garden, you will want to give them a place to collect water such as a pond, fountain, or a bee bath. A bee bath is a simple bee waterer that is easy to make and care for in your home garden, and it's a nice touch to set one out for your pollinating guests.

A shallow dish or bowl with some rocks in it that sits above clean water is just enough to give bees a drink. The idea is to create a source of fresh water that has places for bees to perch as they drink and collect water.

Materials
Shallow dish
Plant pot
River stones
Fresh water

Make It!

1 Choose a spot in the garden where it is protected and shady.

2 Turn a plant pot upside down to use as a base, and set a shallow dish on top of the pot. Choose a dish that is water-safe such as glass or ceramic, as plastics and metals may leach into the water.

3 Add a few river stones to the dish and just enough water so that the tops of the stones are not submerged.

4 Change the water daily and clean the bee bath weekly with Castile soap.

Keeping It Clean

While it's a whole lot of fun to serve recipes of homemade goodies to backyard wildlife, it also comes with some responsibility. Feeders and bird-baths need to be regularly maintained and cleaned to keep garden visitors safe. Just because the recipes are served outdoors doesn't mean you can just set them and forget them. Harmful microorganisms can grow and make wildlife sick. Follow the maintenance and cleaning steps outlined in each project to keep critters happy and safe.

Backyard Birdseed Recipes

As every backyard bird parent knows, they sure can go through a lot of seed! If you've ever bought bags of mixed birdseed for your feathered friends, then you have undoubtedly had to deal with a big mess of dropped seeds below your feeder. Not all birds like all seeds, and those big bags of standard mix are often filled with low-cost filler that the birds quickly toss out to get to the good stuff. Making your own seed mix will save a few extra bucks while tailoring the mix to the birds you want to visit.

Come One, Come All All-Purpose Mix

Materials
Black oil sunflower
Safflower
Shelled peanuts
Millet
Nyjer seed

This mix has a variety of seed to attract common feeder birds, including ground birds that hop around below the feeder keeping the ground clean(ish). Start with a mix of all the seeds, and if you see any of the ingredients being tossed out and left behind, eliminate those on the next round. Note that you may have different birds visiting in winter as you do in summer; the mix can be adjusted seasonally.

No Mess Mix *(No Shells)*

Materials
Hulled sunflower
seeds
Shelled peanuts
Tree nuts (chopped)
Hulled millet

Shelled seeds and nuts are a lot less messy because there aren't any shells discarded below the feeder. This mix will attract a variety of backyard birds to your garden.

Trail Mix *(Seeds and Fruit)*

Materials
Black oil sunflower
Safflower
Shelled peanuts
Millet
Fruit, such as apple
slices, grapes,
cranberries

Birds appreciate a mix of seeds and fruit for a balanced meal. Fruit can be either fresh or dried but do not use any with added sugar or additives. Fresh fruit such as apple slices, grapes, and cranberries are enjoyed by birds and will last well in the winter garden if the temperature is cold.

The Class Clowns *(Peanuts in the Shell)*

Materials
Peanuts in the shell

Add peanuts in the shell to a feeder with large holes hanging from a wire to watch large birds, like jays and crows, and critters like squirrels perform acrobatics to try and wrangle the peanuts out. When they tire out, the smaller birds like chickadees will come in and sensibly peck at the shells to release the peanuts.

High Fat Winter Suet

In winter, suet is a great way to attract insect-eating birds, such as woodpeckers, chickadees, nuthatches, and jays. The high fat and protein sources are important to keep birds going through winter so they will be energetic and ready for pest patrol duties in spring.

Suet Recipe

½ cup (120 ml) rendered fat

¼ (60 ml) cup peanut butter

1 cup (235 ml) birdseed mix

¼ cup (60 ml) rolled oats

Materials

Suet

Enamel camping mug

6-inch-long (15-cm-long) twig

Duct tape

Metal key chain ring

Make It!

1 Use duct tape to attach the twig to the inside of an enamel camping mug, on the opposite side of the handle.

2 Melt the rendered fat in a Mason jar set in a pot of hot water. Stir in the peanut butter, birdseed, and oats.

3 Pour the suet mixture into the mug and set it in the refrigerator or freezer to set.

4 Hang the feeder from a strong branch using the metal key chain clip, which will hold firmly through winter.

1

Hummingbird Nectar

Materials
1 part sugar
4 parts water

Visiting hummingbirds are one of the greatest garden delights. The sound of their wings, the speed of their movements, the shimmer of their feathers—all this makes them a highly attractive garden guest. If you don't have enough reasons to love them, they also fill their belly with aphids, mosquitoes, gnats, whiteflies, and insect eggs. Invite them for a sweet cocktail and they will happily reward you with pest control and silly antics.

Make It!

1 Boil the sugar and water together in a pot and allow it to cool.

2 Fill the feeder with the nectar and replace and clean the feeder every 2 to 3 days in warm weather, once a week in cool weather.

3 Store any leftover nectar in the refrigerator for a week.

No Additives or Substitutions, Please

While some store-bought nectar has red dye added, please do not add food coloring as it can harm the birds. Instead, use a feeder with some red on it to attract hummingbirds. It's also important to note that while we often hear of sugar alternatives that are better for human consumption, plain white sugar is best for hummingbird food and it should not be replaced with maple syrup, honey, brown sugar, coconut sugar, stevia, or any other sugar substitute.

Aphid Nursery

As you may have naturally discovered, there are some plants in your garden that aphids just love. Nasturtium, feverfew, Shasta daisy, broad beans, kale, linden, fruit trees—aphids aren't picky about whether it's an herb, flower, shrub, or tree; they just want to suck that sweet sap and have babies.

One of the best ways to keep aphids from taking over your garden is to plant some of their favorite plants. Why would I ever suggest creating an area in your garden to attract pests? Before you throw this book out the window, please hear me out. Pest populations need to reach a certain threshold in order for predatory insects to make patrolling your garden worth their while. Creating an aphid "nursery" allows you to control the location of the aphids and thus attract chickadees, wasps, hoverflies, and ladybugs to keep the rest of the plants aphid-free.

If you find yourself getting concerned about those little leaf suckers all over your plants, just remember that you don't have an aphid infestation; you have ladybug scarcity. Creating a garden that can be enjoyed by all creatures is a much larger joy than perfectly pristine plants.

Make It!

Plant sacrificial perennials or annuals that aphids are known to love away from your prized plants. Some of the plants that aphids love, including nasturtiums, mustards, kale, Shasta daisies, and feverfew, are hardy enough to stand up to their abuse. Plant these early in the season, before the peak growing season of your prized plants. This will ensure that there is enough time to attract predators before your other plants become too attractive to aphids. Monitor the success of the nursery through managing the population of aphids. Aphids multiply quickly, so the numbers can quickly get out of hand while you wait for predators. If the aphids start to take over more than 20 percent of the plant, remove some of the aphids with pruning or a water spray.

Farmer Ants

Ants love to "farm" aphids for the sweet honeydew they produce. Ants aren't harmful to plants, but they will protect the aphids from predators. If ants are becoming a detriment to the predatory insects, then hose off the aphids every day for a week or two; the ants will eventually move on to another food source that isn't so much trouble.

The Humble Garden Hose

You don't have to bring out the big guns for tiny armies of insects feeding on your plants. In many cases, the jet spray from your garden hose is enough to keep pest populations under control. Aphids, spider mites, and spittlebugs love to sip the sap from your plants, but a quick spray will send them flying. The spray will dislodge the insects and change the environment, making it less desirable. Spider mites detest wet conditions and so regular spraying will send them packing. Aphids won't be able to make a trip back up the plant. Some aphids are born without legs (just mouth parts and reproductive organs to eat and make more aphids, yuck), so a spray of water is very effective at removing them.

Adopt a Predator (Dog, Chicken, Duck, and So On!)

One of the best ways to introduce beneficial predators into your garden is to adopt them! Chickens, ducks, and dogs are hard-working garden hands that are happily paid in food, shelter, and belly rubs. If you have the space and ability to add livestock such as chickens or ducks, they will waddle around your garden and gobble up slugs, grasshoppers, beetles, and more. Dogs can be helpful at pest control as well. While indoors they may catch and snack on a few rogue houseflies and mosquitoes, but what's even more helpful is their desire to mark (with urine) to protect their territory, which deters animal pests. While each breed and individual animal is different, even the presence of a dog should be enough to send mice, rats, rabbits, raccoons, squirrels, and skunks looking for lodging and food elsewhere. Dogs also bark and chase unwanted garden visitors away.

Coyote, wolf, fox, bear, cougar, and other large animal urine is sold as a pest barrier that can be applied to your property. The odor of the urine is meant to deter animals such as deer, weasels, and armadillos. It's sold in granules or liquid form that is applied to your property every month or reapplied after heavy rains. Given the yuck factor in the application and the questionable source of the ingredients, adopting a dog is a much better option.

Fungus Gnat Sand

Fungus gnats, sometimes called soil gnats, resemble small fruit flies and infest houseplants. Fungus gnats can get into your houseplants when they are left outside, but usually, they come straight from the nursery, where they hide in the soil until you bring them home unknowingly. Their larvae eat fungi and plant roots in the soil and then hatch, which is why they suddenly appear in houseplants that were otherwise pest-free.

Preventing gnats is pretty simple. By removing their habitat, changing your watering habits, and adding a layer of fungus gnat sand, you'll have gnats no more.

Materials

Choose any of the following or combine a mix of them:

Coarse sand

Crushed gravel

Decorative aquarium rocks

Make It!

1 Let the soil dry completely, then scrape off the top inch (2.5 cm) of soil and discard it.

2 Add a layer of any one or a mix of these materials to replace the top layer of soil.

3 Water the plant by filling the bottom tray and allowing the water to wick up into the soil.

Discard any water that isn't wicked up within 30 minutes to prevent the soil from becoming oversaturated.

Store Extra Potting Soil in an Airtight Container

If you keep your potting soil in a bag or open bucket, fungus gnats can easily get in and lay their eggs, but the eggs need air to survive so airtight containers like buckets with tight-fitting lids will keep gnat larvae at bay.

Herbal Pest Deterrent Spray

Make a homemade herbal pest-be-gone spray using fresh herbs, water, and a bit of soap to allow the spray to adhere to leaves.

Garlic and red pepper are often ingredients in commercial natural deterrents for insects, birds, and animals like deer and rabbits. The combination of the odor of the spray and the taste isn't harmful to the pests, but it does tend to send them elsewhere for food.

Materials

6 whole, unpeeled cloves of garlic

1 or 2 whole spicy chili peppers

½ cup (120 ml) chopped herbs from "Herbs that Repel Pests" (optional)

Blender

Mason jar with a lid

Nut milk bag

Rubber gloves

¼ teaspoon (1 ml) liquid Castile soap

Make It!

1 Add the garlic cloves and chili peppers (including seeds) into a blender. Prepare fresh or dried herbs by removing the leaves and/or flowers and composting any woody stems.

2 Cover with water to fill the blender half-full and blend until thoroughly liquified. Add more water to fill the blender two-thirds of the way full, and blend again.

3 Strain the mixture through a nut milk bag, and squeeze to release all of the liquid. Wear gloves to protect your hands when squeezing the liquid from the nut milk bag to avoid a skin reaction.

4 Add a small amount of unscented Castile soap and stir. Castile soap can often come in a liquid concentrate, so dilute it as per the package instructions before using.

5 Pour the liquid into a spray bottle and shake before each use.

Caution: Always test a small amount of any homemade concoction on a part of one plant to watch for any reaction. Discontinue use if plants show any negative response.

HERBS THAT REPEL PESTS

Many herbs deter specific pests from feasting on plants. Add the plants from this list to the garlic and chili blend or use them to make your own custom recipe. Note that some of these herbs could also deter beneficial insects and wildlife from your garden. Use them only when pest populations need intervention and discontinue use as soon as the balance is restored.

HERB	BOTANICAL NAME	REPELS
BASIL	*Ocimum basilicum*	Whiteflies, carrot fly, asparagus beetle
BORAGE	*Borago officinalis*	Tomato hornworm, asparagus beetles
CATNIP	*Nepeta cataria*	Ants, flea beetles, aphids, Japanese beetle, squash bugs, weevils, Colorado potato beetle, cabbage looper, cockroaches Note: Attracts cats.
CHIVES	*Allium schoenoprasum*	Carrot fly, Japanese beetle, aphids
CILANTRO/CORIANDER	*Coriandrum sativum*	Aphids, spider mites, Colorado potato beetle
DILL	*Anethum graveolens*	Aphids, squash bugs, spider mites, cabbage looper
LAVENDER	*Lavandula* spp.	Moths, fleas, flies, mosquitoes
MINT	*Mentha* spp.	Ants, aphids, cabbage looper, flea beetles, squash bugs, whiteflies
PENNYROYAL	*Mentha pulegium*	Ants, gnats, fleas, mosquitoes, flies, mice
ROSEMARY	*Rosmarinus officinalis*	Cabbage looper, carrot fly, cockroaches, mosquitoes, slugs, snails, Mexican bean beetle
RUE	*Ruta graveolens*	Cucumber and flea beetles
TANSY	*Tanacetum vulgare*	Ants, beetles, flies, squash bugs, cutworms, Small White, Cabbage White
TOMATO LEAF	*Lycopersicon esculentum*	Many insects
WORMWOOD	*Artemisia absinthium*	Ants, earwigs, flies, fleas, slugs, cabbage looper, cabbage maggot, carrot fly, moths, flea beetles, whiteflies, mice

Citronella Flower Pot Candle to Repel Mosquitoes

Citronella candles are a great companion to keep mosquitoes at bay. For the common garden variety mosquitoes that come out at dusk, placing a few scented candles around a space will add ambiance for you and mask your scent from mosquitoes. If you live where there are no mosquito-borne diseases or a serious overpopulation of mosquitoes, this system works well to deter these bloodsuckers without the need to douse your skin or clothing with insecticide.

Materials

6-inch (15-cm) terracotta flower pot

Outdoor silicone sealer

Electrical tape

Sheet of cork

Mod Podge

Paintbrush

1 lb. (450 g) soy wax for the container candles

Three HTP 1312 6-inch (15-cm) waxed and wired wicks with tabs

1 oz. (28 ml) pure citronella oil

Equipment

Hot glue gun and glue

Double boiler

Thermometer

Kitchen scale

Paper cup

Chopsticks or clothespins

Using three wicks in a large terracotta flower pot will create more smoke and a larger pool of wax to release the citronella oil. The combination of smoke and citronella scent in your yard may be enough that the mosquitoes search elsewhere for a food source.

Make It!

1 Measure the radius of the pot and place the three wicks evenly spaced at half the radius. Imagine that three candles are set in the pot together; the wick would be in the center of each one. Use hot glue to affix the wick tabs to the bottom of the pot.

2 Look for a terracotta flower pot without a drainage hole if you can find one. If not, then cover the inside of the hole with electrical tape and fill the hole with an outdoor silicone sealer. When the sealer is dry, cut a circle of cork to cover the base of the pot and use hot glue to attach it in place.

3 Prepare the flower pot by painting the inside of the pot with a non-flammable sealer like Mod Podge. Allow the sealer to dry according to the package instructions.

4 Melt the soy wax in the top of a double boiler and bring to 160°F (71°C).

5 Add the citronella oil and stir well.

6 Cool to 140°F (60°C) and pour into the flower pot until it's ½ inch (1 cm) from the top.

7 Prop the wicks up straight with chopsticks.

8 Allow the wax to dry completely untouched in a warm room. When dry, trim the wicks to ¼ inch (0.6 cm) above the wax.

Note: Be sure to set the candle on a heat-proof base to protect surfaces from heat or leaks or when burning.

Make Your Garden a Mosquito-Free Zone

Mosquitoes can be a nuisance in the garden, but they don't travel far. Keep the garden clean and remove standing water and you shouldn't have too many of them to contend with.

If you live in an area that is endemic to mosquito-borne disease, then please protect yourself with WHO-approved topical repellants and clothing. (WHO stands for World Health Organization.)

Recycled Bottle Trap for Flies, Wasps, and Stink Bugs

This recycled bottle trap's simple yet ingenious design is easy to make with a humble plastic bottle from the recycling bin. The design makes it easy for pests to enter, but they can't find their way out. The trap can be customized to attract different pests depending on the bait you use to lure them.

1   2   3

Make It!

1 Cut a plastic bottle all the way around the diameter approximately one-third from the top with scissors or a box cutter.

2 Invert the top of the bottle and set it inside the cut bottom part of the bottle.

3 Add 1 inch (2.5 cm) of the insect bait recipe of your choice to the bottom part of the bottle. Be sure that there is at least 1 inch (2.5 cm) of water or liquid to drown the insects, but that there is solid food poking out above the water.

Insect Bait Recipes

House Flies

Flies enjoy rotting meat and decaying material. Add raw meat or fish and water to the trap. Set it in a sunny location where flies are prevalent. The sun will quickly spoil the meat and release the perfect aroma to attract flies.

Wasps

Wasps look for protein sources early in life and switch to preferring sugary treats at the end of their life cycle. At the beginning of wasp season, place cooked or raw meat or fish in an inch of water. At the end of the season, dilute some jam or mashed fruit in a bit of water.

Brown Marmorated Stink Bugs

Place a small, battery-operated LED light at the bottom of the bottle and set it in a dark place. If the light is waterproof, you can add water to drown the stink bugs. (If the light is not waterproof, don't use water.) They still won't be able to get out of the trap, but you will have live stink bugs to contend with in the morning.

Slug Bait

Slugs and snails vigorously decimate tender, leafy plants such as lettuce, cabbage, and hosta along with these other vegetable garden favorites: strawberries, cucumbers, and zucchini. They can mow through a salad garden faster than you can pick, sneaking out at night while you are tucked in bed.

The one thing slugs seem to like even more than plants is beer. Technically, it's the yeast in the beer that they love, so before you pop open a brew for the slugs, you can make your own slug bait and a DIY trap from much less precious ingredients.

Materials
2 cups (475 ml) warm water
1 packet dry yeast
1 teaspoon (5 ml) sugar

Make It!

Combine all the ingredients and stir well. Add the mixture to the DIY slug trap.

DIY Slug Trap

Materials

Plastic container with a lid

Box cutter

Slug bait

Make It!

Use whatever container you have on hand to make this trap—it can be a yogurt or dairy container, take-out box, coffee cup—anything that will hold up in the soil and has a lid. Cut out a few openings in the top one-third of the container. Bury the container so that the openings are at soil level. Fill the container with slug bait and attach the lid.

Check the trap daily to remove slugs and monitor the slug population. At first you should capture the big ones, and after a few days, it will be just the smaller ones. When no more slugs are caught in the trap, pack it up for a few weeks and use it again if you notice more slug activity.

Fruit Fly Trap

This fruit fly trap works like a dream whenever there is an abundance of fruit flies. Set it in your kitchen, worm bin, or compost pile, and the fruit flies won't have a fighting chance.

Materials
Small glass bowl
Wine or juice
Ripe fruit
Natural dish soap
Plastic wrap
Bamboo skewer

3

4

Make It!

1 Fill a small glass bowl with the wine or juice and a piece of ripe fruit. If you use just plain syrup or vinegar, it will not work as well. Fruit flies are looking for rotting fruit to lay eggs in.

2 Put a few drops of dish soap in the liquid.

3 Cover tightly with a piece of plastic wrap and poke a few holes in it with a bamboo skewer. Make sure the holes are big enough that fruit flies can find their way in.

4 Remove all temptation from the area (i.e.: move the offending fruit) and place the trap in its spot. Clean the trap when it's full and repeat if the problem persists.

Resources

Cornell University School of Integrative Plant Science-Horticulture Resources, www.hort.cals.cornell.edu

Earth User's Guide to Permaculture, Rosemary Morrow (2010)

Gaia's Garden: A Guide to Home-Scale Permaculture, Second Edition, Toby Hemenway (2009)

National Audubon Society www.audubon.org

National Wildlife Federation Attracting Birds, Butterflies, and Other Backyard Wildlife, Dan Mizejewski (2019) https://www.nwf.org/

Permaculture Design Notes, Edited by Delvin Solkinson with Kym Chi (2017), www.permaculturedesign.ca

Permaculture Research Institute https://permaculturenews.org/

Permaculture: A Designers' Manual, Bill Mollison and Reny Mia Slayug (1997)

Practical Organic Gardening: The No-Nonsense Guide to Growing Naturally, Mark Highland (2017)

Richter's Herbs, www.richters.com

Teaming with Microbes: A Gardener's Guide to the Soil Food Web, Jeff Lowenfels and Wayne Lewis (2010)

Teaming with Nutrients: The Organic Gardener's Guide to Optimizing Plant Nutrition, Jeff Lowenfels (2013)

The Rodale Institute, www.rodaleinstitutre.org

West Coast Seeds, www.westcoastseeds.com

Acknowledgments

I'm forever grateful for the opportunity to learn from people and places that celebrate nature and gardens. To the Vancouver Master Gardeners; Stacy Friedman, the UBC Farm, and the Intergenerational Landed Learning Program; Kym Chi of PermacultureDesign.ca; Lori Snyder educator and herbalist at LoriSnyder.co; Meg and those who farm at the Yarrow EcoVillage; A Rocha Farm; Pau Farré, Mike, and City Farmer; the members of the Strathcona Community Garden; the Bloedel Conservatory; VanDusen Gardens; GardenWorks; and the Sharing Farm Society, thank you for sharing your wisdom.

This book wouldn't have been possible without the amazing team at Cool Springs Press who worked with me to bring this idea to paper. My editor, Jessica Walliser, is full of brilliant advice and guidance, not to mention the garden-geekery to love worm poop like I do. Mark, Steve, Heather, John, the talented creative team, and everyone who I have had the pleasure to work with has brought so much experience and vision.

While writing a book one spends much time alone with words, but I was never truly alone with author friends like Shawna Coronado, Devon Young, Tara Nolan, and Niki Jabbour cheering me on while photographers Susan Goble, Crystal Allen, and Michael Rose captured me in my happy place. My biggest fans, Elisabeth, Bill, and Marie, are always there, championing creativity and providing me with mountains of support while buying stacks of my books to give as gifts.

I'm humbly appreciative to my Garden Therapy friends and readers who take the time to send me supportive messages and leave their thoughtful words on my website to help the community learn through their experience as well. With that, I would like to say a huge THANK YOU to you for buying or borrowing this book. I hope you have enjoyed it and if you did, please tell a friend or give it as a gift. Keep spreading the word of the beauty and magic of gardening so we all may have the joy of learning through plants.

About the Author

STEPHANIE ROSE is an award-winning author, freelance writer, instructor, and international speaker who aims to encourage healing and wellness through gardening. She is both a long-time student and teacher of organic gardening, permaculture, herbalism, and natural skin care formulation. She has multiple certificates in permaculture and herbalism; is a member of Permaculture Institute of North America, Garden Communicators International, and the International Herb Association; and she volunteers to develop children's gardens as a Vancouver Master Gardener.

Stephanie is the founder of the popular website Garden Therapy (GardenTherapy.ca) and has written several books, including *Home Apothecary* (Leisure Arts, 2018), *The Natural Beauty Recipe Book* (Rose Garden Press, 2016), and *Garden Made: A Year of Seasonal Projects to Beautify Your Garden and Your Life* (Roost Books, 2015), which was a Gold Medal Winner from the 2016 Independent Publishers Book Awards (the "IPPYs").

Stephanie spends her time as a gardener, writer, and photographer in Vancouver, BC, Canada. She is passionate about organic gardening, natural healing, and

Stephanie Rose, **award-winning author and creator of Garden Therapy (GardenTherapy.ca)**

art as part of life. Stephanie lives with her family and a motley crew of animals, which provide her with inspiration and delight both in and out of the garden.

Visit Stephanie online at www.GardenTherapy.ca.

Index